The Black Student's Guide
to High School Success

THE BLACK STUDENT'S GUIDE TO HIGH SCHOOL SUCCESS

Edited by **William J. Ekeler**

Foreword by **L. Douglas Wilder**
**Former Governor of
the State of Virginia**

Greenwood Press
Westport, Connecticut • London

Library of Congress Cataloging-in-Publication Data

The Black student's guide to high school success / edited by William
    J. Ekeler ; foreword by L. Douglas Wilder.
        p.   cm.
    ISBN 0–313–29848–3 (alk. paper)
    1. Afro-Americans—Education (Secondary)—Handbooks, manuals, etc.
    2. Afro-American students—Handbooks, manuals, etc.   3. High school
    students—United States—Handbooks, manuals, etc.   I. Ekeler,
    William J.
    LC2779.B53   1997
    373.18'089'96073—dc20   96–32982

British Library Cataloguing in Publication Data is available.

Library of Congress Catalog Card Number: 96–32982
ISBN: 0–313–29848–3

First published in 1997

Greenwood Press, 88 Post Road West, Westport, CT 06881
An imprint of Greenwood Publishing Group, Inc.

Printed in the United States of America

The paper used in this book complies with the
Permanent Paper Standard issued by the National
Information Standards Organization (Z39.48–1984).

10 9 8 7 6 5 4 3 2 1

Contents

Foreword

THE HONORABLE L. DOUGLAS WILDER
Former Governor of the State of Virginia

So many people said I could never sit behind the desk of the office that I hold today, but I never believed them. They said the time was not right or my goals were too lofty, but I ignored their pessimism. I have always known that I can achieve whatever heights I desire as long as my hard work and determination match my ambition.

Many people, past and present, inspired me along the way. I found great strength in the men I was named for: Frederick Douglass, an abolitionist-orator of great courage, who did not allow his status as a slave to prevent him from succeeding; and Paul Laurence Dunbar, a poet of great eloquence, who gave voice to the emotions and dreams of people long left silent, and expressed, in many forms, the plight of his people.

Likewise, the men and women I have met in public life have always inspired me. I firmly believe that public service is the rent people pay on this earth for our rewards beyond, and to be in touch with the people and to serve their will has been one of my greatest joys in life.

Public figures like Thurgood Marshall, Oliver Hill, Spottswood Robinson III, Arthur Ashe, Reggie Lewis, and others who overcame discrimination and blazed paths for us all have been a great inspiration as well.

But without a doubt, the person who gave me the greatest strength and determination in my life was my mother. Because of her, all of the obstacles I have faced in life have seemed less daunting, and none of the achievements have been too self-gratifying.

Although my mother never completed high school, she knew the importance of education and expected her children to do well in school. An A in school was not something to be rewarded, but rather something to be expected.

Her concern about my siblings' and my education extended beyond the school walls. She insisted that I continue to develop my vocabulary, no matter what I had to learn in school. Every day she would choose a new word for me to learn, often out of her daily crossword puzzles.

At the end of the week, she would test me on the words, asking me to give the definition of each. My mother's Aunt Kate contributed to our education as well. She would hold formal "tea parties" in which all of the children were expected to perform—singing, playing an instrument, or reciting poetry.

We learned more than our various interests and talents; we also learned social graces that you can't pick up on a playground. This isn't to say that I didn't enjoy sports, because I spent much of my spare time honing my competitive instincts on the courts and playing fields. Young people today should realize that sports can make you a success, not by making you like Michael Jordan but by teaching you to play hard and to work with others.

Within the segregated school system of the 1940s, there was a definite disadvantage for black students. My elementary school lacked basic facilities such as indoor toilets, a cafeteria, an auditorium, or even a library.

My high school received its textbooks from the local white high school after the students there were finished with them. With only two black high schools in Richmond, they had to stretch their already limited resources to provide for fourteen hundred students. We simply did not have the resources and facilities that were available to the other students.

Compensating for the deficiencies within the school system was the determination of our teachers, parents, and community, who insisted that we work hard and do well in school. Through their support and involvement in our education, we were given a strong base from which to grow.

I have built my entire life upon this base, and it is a foundation that supports me until this day. It carried me off to fight for my country in the Korean War, through Howard University Law School, and into a successful law practice.

Mostly, it has helped me know my own self-worth when others have doubted. Through your life, expect many to say that you are not smart enough or that you don't work hard enough. Don't ignore what they say, but don't take it to heart either.

If you set standards for yourself to learn all you can, to ask questions and speak up when you disagree, you'll do more than prove the skeptics wrong. You'll learn how to beat them at their own game.

There is no stronger man or woman than the one whom others assume is weak; there is no wiser man or woman than the one whom others discount or ignore.

Whatever people tell you that you cannot do, remember their words and work that much harder to prove them wrong. And always remember the loving words and support of those who know you best and want you to reach the heights.

Preface

RICHARD ARRINGTON, JR.

Mayor, City of Birmingham, Alabama

Life for me began in 1934 in a little place in the road near Livingston, Alabama. I am the older of two sons born to Ernestine and Richard Arrington, Sr.

My father was a sharecropper. As was the case with a number of black sharecroppers, life was a constant struggle. I ought to add that the concept of sharecropping holds that the landowner provides his "wage hands" with a modest place to stay, usually on his property. In return for the worker's labor on the farm, he and his family would share the results of the yields from various crops, usually cotton. "Share" does not mean a 50–50 split of the profits! The landowner bought the seeds, fertilizers, mules, and so on, and wage hands worked the land. Meanwhile, the worker (my father) would from time to time need cash and foodstuffs. He got these things from the landowner. They were put on "the book" and subtracted from what my father was entitled to at settlement time, usually in late autumn. The reality is that each year, farm hands operating within such an arrangement would end up owing "the man." Hence, he was locked in. He could not leave until he paid his debts. This went on for years.

My father decided to move his family to Birmingham to join his brother who had moved there years earlier. So, my family gathered up its meager belongings and set out for the land of improved life—Birmingham, Alabama.

My father was a talented man who could do many things, especially with his hands. In fact, during his leisure time he built the home that my mother currently occupies. But his late talents were not in demand in the "iron house" at Tennessee Coal, Iron and Land Company. He worked there for over thirty-five years and did odd jobs to supplement his family's income. I ought to add that my father was a bit suspicious of banks. He would save his money in a shoe box which he placed in the loft of the house. This practice he observed even when we lived in a three-room shotgun house in Birmingham. My father and some of our neighbors completed our family home during the mid-1950s.

I attended Fairfield Industrial High School, which, by its name, was intended to prepare coloreds to get a job using their muscles primarily. Our school had an academic side and a good principal. More on that later.

I was a serious student, and learning came fairly easily. However, my mother was a stern taskmaster who vowed that my brother and I would devote ourselves to learning all that we could. She literally took a razor strap to me when she felt that I was not applying myself to knowing all that was in the tattered books that we were forced to employ, perhaps castoffs from the white school system.

My grades were sufficient that I was passed from the third grade to the fifth grade.

I got to high school and met E. J. Oliver, who changed my life. Professor Oliver, the principal, was committed to educating us to be good, productive citizens. He kept order, using the lash and psychology as enforcers. He was single-minded in his efforts to get equipment for the school that would enable us to be all that we could become. He enjoyed the support of the parents of students at my school. He challenged parents to support our school and to join his faculty in a partnership for the production of better, more informed students. Oliver taught race pride, not as a negative but as a vital tool that would engender self-respect and a sense of personal worth and dignity in all of us. Achievement was a tradition at my school.

Completing high school in 1951, I enrolled at Miles College, which was less than a block from my house. Realizing that there was little money to go toward my education at some distant and prestigious college that was away from the city of Birmingham, I went to Miles with the understanding that I had to pay for my college education. Fortunately, I had taken dry cleaning as a skill at Fairfield Industrial High School, so I got a job at a local laundry where I worked after school and on weekends for a number of years—even into adulthood.

At Miles College, a small, underfunded Christian Methodist Episcopal School, I began to blossom. The faculty at Miles inspired me to study hard and to put aside my natural shyness and become involved in extracurricular activities such as student government. The school's president, Dr. W. A. Bell, was especially influential in my development, as were Emmit Jones, my major professor, and Mrs. Verdell Day Martin, who told me that I possessed the tools to succeed if I applied myself. I believed her. Finishing Miles near the top of my class, I, with the assistance of Emmit Jones who attended the same graduate school, got a scholarship to the University of Detroit, as I sought a master's degree in biology. Now came the firm test of my intellect. By then, I was married with children.

I dreaded being in an all-white learning environment. Self-doubt nearly overwhelmed me! My fear was that if called on in class I would not know the answer and I would thus let the entire black race down. For days I avoided being assertive. I was called on one day and summoned all of the courage I could muster and responded—correctly, as I recall. By now, my confidence was edging toward full throttle. I finished graduate school on time and returned to Miles College as a member of its faculty. During the early 1960s, and some children later, I went to the University of Oklahoma in pursuit of a doctorate. There I was in another strange, primarily white environment. There were few other blacks there in any capacity. On campus in Norman, Oklahoma, our problems as blacks were minimal, but off campus, being black was not socially and otherwise advantageous. I felt the way Jackie Robinson must have felt. But I was determined to achieve the goals I had for being at the university. I did, and after earning a doctorate, I returned to Birmingham. I was again given a position at Miles College and was later named dean of Instruction and head of the Department of Natural Science. But while I was away in school, the city of Birmingham erupted, as the demonstrations led by Dr. Martin Luther King, Jr., spread in Birmingham and were front-page news in the entire world. I missed being active during that period, and to this day, I experience feelings of guilt that I was not a greater, more active instrument of change. I am comforted by the fact that as mayor of this city I have more than made up for my absence during the heat of the battle to tame Birmingham.

Some friends persuaded me to run for the Birmingham City Council. I did, after much thought and encouragement from my parents, and I won. I served a four-year term from 1971 to 1975 and another from 1975 to 1979. During this time, I sought, within the scope of my influence as a city councilor, to bring justice and fairness to black citizens, especially in the realms of putting an end to police mistreatment of black citizens and equal employment opportunities in hiring by city government.

A black female was shot by a white police officer during the summer of 1979, and, once again, black citizens began to respond with demonstrations of their discontent with the way blacks were generally treated by the police in the local courts. There were several nights of violence in the neighborhood where the young woman was killed. Some local citizens began to look for someone to run for mayor in order to turn out the incumbent mayor, who refused to take sufficiently strong action against the police officer who fired the fatal shots. Some of my former students and some local ministers persuaded me to run for mayor. I declined, but they insisted. I ran and after a runoff, I won. There finally was a mayor of all of the people of Birmingham, a black mayor of Birmingham, a city that had a history of racial bigotry—Birmingham, a city that was once compared with Johannesburg, South Africa.

I set about to do my duty. It was hardly easy. The police department at that time did all that it could do to take away my authority and to reduce my effectiveness. I would articulate a policy of change in the morning, and some of the leadership of the largely white police department would call a news conference in the afternoon to rail against it. Amid bomb threats and poor cooperation from law enforcement and some department heads, we set about to govern.

Anyone who looks at Birmingham today will concede that it is a changed city. The mostly white police department is integrated, and now it is headed by a black police chief. Blacks hold rank from patrolman to chief and deputy chief. Many of the department heads of the city are now black. During the last twelve years as mayor, I have appointed twenty-two department heads—eleven blacks and eleven whites. During my administration, we have been able to fashion programs that enable blacks to share the economic blessings of this city.

In November 1992, the city of Birmingham opened a $12 million Civil Rights Institute that is an indicator of how far Birmingham has come. Race relations in our city, though a long way from being perfect, are considerably improved.

My father, who was at all times my hero, always told me to do a good job no matter the task. He taught me to have pride and to believe in the fact that hard work is redemptive. Professor Oliver and W. A. Bell of Miles College; Lucius Pitts, once president of Miles College; and my church taught me that I had a responsibility to use whatever tools at my disposal for the common good.

The youth of this nation ought to know that if their will is sufficiently strong, if they seek knowledge and value their own worth, they too can come out all right. It is my judgment that being a productive citizen is not restricted to those who are highly educated. Some of the best, most influential people I know are those males and females of limited formal education, who speak broken English but who love their families, take care of their responsibilities, and seek to meet the needs of someone other than themselves. Hence, there is no shortage of heroes in our racial group. Sadly, many people who look for role models fail to note the endless numbers of just plain, decent folks who are honest, hard-working, law-abiding, compassionate individuals—vital resources that abound in every community.

Introduction

You have been looking for guidance and ways to improve your future. Picking up this book is an excellent first step in expanding your knowledge about future success—more specifically, your future success in high school. The purpose of this book is to take young black students in a step-by-step manner through the process of completing a high school education. The book offers candid advice on how to get the most out of your high school education by making intelligent, informed decisions in and out of the classroom.

Black students should be excited about the opportunities that lie ahead. The Bureau of Census has reported that high school dropout rates among African Americans decreased from 26.5 percent in 1973 to 16.4 percent in 1993. In addition, the number of black high school graduates was up from 60.4 percent in 1975 to 69.6 percent in 1993. The Bureau of Census also reports that college enrollment for black students who have graduated from high school in the preceding twelve months is on the rise. In 1976 only 41.8 percent of black high school graduates attended college, while in 1993 the number increased to 47.9 percent. Of those blacks who chose to attend college, 60 percent selected four-year institutions and 40 percent two-year degree programs or community colleges. This publication will help you keep increasing those numbers and ultimately attend college or successfully enter the workforce.

The *Black Student's Guide to High School Success* is an informative guide written specifically for black junior high and high school students. Students will benefit from fifteen chapters focusing on scholastic and social topics. The book also stresses the importance of the relationship between the two. The focus is not on instructing students on specific choices to make. Rather, it emphasizes providing black students with the necessary background information to make informed decisions.

Fifteen outstanding educators from across the nation were asked to write chapters on various aspects of the high school experience. The writers were instructed to be candid in their advice and to write in a conversational tone, as if the young black student were seated in their office. The authors were asked to write intellectually and to include past experiences whenever applicable. It was my intent to include authors representing geographic diversity, experience, and professional disciplines. This was done to give the reader a greater opportunity to relate to as many philosophies as possible.

Student essays complement each of the fifteen chapters. These essays were written by highly successful black students in their final year of high school or first few years of college. Each essay provides a personal story of what success means to them and how they obtained success as students. These essays are designed to act as road maps for future students. It is my hope that they will encourage the young black reader to strive for excellence.

I strongly urge black students of all ages and ability levels to read this book carefully. While reading it, keep in mind the positive strides black students have made over the past several years. Use this work not only for the important information it offers, but also as inspiration for your future success. Success takes effort. I challenge you to make the effort, the sacrifices, and the difficult decisions and to work hard to succeed and fulfill your dreams.

CHAPTER 1

Selecting a High School

ROLAND M. ALLEN
Director of Freshman Admissions, Massachusetts Institute of
Technology

WHAT CHOICE?

This is the question the majority of students about to enter
high school will respond with if asked whether they've thought
about choosing a high school. For most students the only
"choice" is to move on to the neighborhood public school that
everyone else will attend. That might be the best option for
you. In fact, we'll discuss the local public high school first. But
read this chapter carefully. You might find that there are more
choices than you've previously thought.

THE LOCAL PUBLIC SCHOOL

The local public high school can offer great opportunity to
most students. It has the advantage of being close to home

and filled with people you already know. Also, and this is important to students of color, it means that you don't have to leave your community for an education. Assuming that the local public high school can offer good courses in many areas and an array of extracurricular activities, this could be a good choice for you. Public schools could have distinct advantages in that most of them are large enough to offer an array of sports and extracurricular clubs.

But what if the local public school is deficient? While this might still remain an educational option for you, there are ways to enhance any educational experience. For example, if you are interested in particular academic areas or more advanced subjects that your high school doesn't offer, you may be able to cross-register in another high school that does offer those subjects. Also, some students find that local junior or senior colleges or universities will allow high school students to register for courses.

You can research these options by talking to teachers in your current school or by going to the counseling office at your local public high school.

MAGNET SCHOOLS

Some school districts have set up special schools to cater to the specific interests of students in their communities. These schools—called magnet schools because they draw students from a large area to a specific place for special interest studies—are a great option if you'd like to learn about a particular academic or professional interest.

The concept of the magnet school was popularized in the movie and TV show *Fame*. Fame was a fictional school in New York City that catered to high school students interested in music and theater. Although most magnet schools won't offer the glamour of Fame, they provide great opportunities within the public sector.

Magnet schools are organized around a theme. Schools that

I am familiar with and have visited offer magnet programs in music and the fine arts, engineering and technologies, mathematics and science, automotive and aeronautical studies, electronics, legal studies, and the health professions. A call to your local school board is the best place to start to research magnet school programs that might be available to you.

MATHEMATICS, SCIENCE, AND TECHNOLOGY ACADEMIES

There has been a surge in public-sponsored mathematics, science, and technology high schools and academies. (These schools are a hybrid of the magnet school concept mentioned earlier. They serve a wider area than one city or school district.) Often these schools represent a partnership between public education at the state level and industry, the professional community, and very often universities. These schools are typically "exam schools." That is, an examination is required for acceptance and entrance into the school. In many cases, too, these schools are residential and will be an option for only a portion of your high school career.

These schools exist in many states and in the Commonwealth of Puerto Rico. They offer an excellent public education. Since many are residential programs, you might have the opportunity of independent living that will give you an experience of college dormitory living. These schools bring together very bright students in a given state with an outstanding faculty. They also have the advantage of being "free" because they are tax supported.

As a note of warning, you may have to leave home midway through high school to attend one of these schools. There may also be a tradeoff for this high-quality education: since these schools are usually smaller, they often won't offer the wide spectrum of sports teams and clubs available at a larger public school.

Yet the advantages make these schools an attractive option.

Some of these schools are located on university campuses. Often the high school students in these schools are able to take advantage of the resources of these universities (libraries, laboratories, etc.) and even classes for college credit. This can be a great head start on college. As a byproduct, it might even save you money by shortening the time you will spend in college. From my perspective as an admissions officer at a major university, I often find that the students who apply for admission at these schools are well prepared, mature, and interesting.

At this writing, just over fifty high schools are member institutions in the National Consortium for Specialized Secondary Schools of Mathematics, Science, and Technology. You can research the central office by writing: NCSSSMST, 417 Washington Street, Arlington, VA 24517.

PAROCHIAL SCHOOLS

While not as popular as they once were, church-related schools are a great option to consider. I read in one publication a few years back that parochial schools are the "poor man's" preparatory schools. Many of these schools were originally set up to serve the educational needs of new immigrants as they came to the United States. They have the advantage of usually being in your community. They're known for offering smaller classes and more personal attention than the local public school, and often they provide a moral education and personal discipline along with solid academics.

Parochial schools have many advantages, but since they are not public supported, there is a tuition charge. My experience has been that the tuition is usually quite reasonable, and that it is reduced or waived based on a family's ability to pay.

You might be surprised at all that might be available to you in the parochial school. Even though they are smaller, I can name a couple dozen small parochial schools with national caliber high school sports teams. These schools are also known for involvement in community service, with many of their curricula featuring a community service component. So, in addition to getting a good education in a supportive environment, you might also have the option of serving your community.

THE AFRO-CENTRIC SCHOOL

Modest growth has taken place in the development of Afro-centric schools, particularly in some midwestern urban centers. Since few such schools exist, there isn't a lot to say about them. Similar to parochial schools, however, Afro-centric schools are noted for discipline and moral formation. There is also the added dimension of learning the history, culture, and practices of African people. Of particular value, an Afro-centric school communicates pride and a sense of self through the school curriculum.

LEAVING HOME

Suburban Schools

In some larger urban communities, a partnership has been struck between city school districts and suburban schools which encourages inner-city students to attend public or private schools in suburban districts. This arrangement serves both communities in that it opens up more opportunities for city youth and their families, and it gives suburban students, who are often white and living in monocultural communities, the opportunity to study with students from different cultural and sometimes socioeconomic backgrounds.

This can be a good option in that it provides a broader academic and cultural experience than you might otherwise have in the local public school. It might also expose you to the better resources of suburban schools. But there are also a few disadvantages to consider. First, there is the disadvantage of travel. Often this option requires substantial commuting time each way, which can limit extracurricular and social involvement outside of school hours. It may also require the social juggling of coming home each day to a community that doesn't share the experiences you're having at your suburban school. These programs go under a number of names, but ask around your school and community to find out if this might be an option for you.

LEAVING SCHOOL

Residential Preparatory Schools

Since I work and live in New England, I'm well aware of residential preparatory schools, or boarding schools, as they are most often called. These schools exist in all areas of the country, not just in New England. This option might not be as far-fetched as you might think.

From my experience, boarding schools bring together an interesting and diverse group of students. The more prominent schools in New England are very proud of their track records in creating and maintaining diverse communities. They bring students together from all over the world, and they're not just for rich kids! These schools are extremely interested in diversity and mount aggressive recruitment campaigns to attract students from different racial and economic backgrounds.

Some cities have organizations that help black students get in touch with these schools. For example, New York City has an organization, Prep-for-Prep, which identifies black students in grade schools and grooms them for New England boarding schools. In Washington, D.C., and Baltimore, the Black Student Fund does similar work. Boston is home for A Better Chance (ABC), which seeks to place minority students in a variety of settings around the country, including boarding schools.

   Ask around your community for options that might be available to you. You might ask at your church, or at the local branch of the NAACP or the Urban League. Or check with the educational committees of community organizations such as Jack and Jill or 100 Black Men. I think you'll be surprised by what's out there.

ENHANCEMENTS TO A HIGH SCHOOL EXPERIENCE

Regardless of your high school choice, the experience can and should be enhanced. As mentioned in the first part of this chapter, you can extend the offerings of your high school experience by taking courses at an area two- or four-year college. In addition, if you have a special interest, you should consider some involvement in that interest. For example, if you are interested in science, you should look for opportunities to do research at a university or in industry.

   You can add a lot to your high school experience by considering a summer program. There are numerous such programs, including guides to summer programs for high school students in your community library. You can buy your own guide to summer programs sponsored on college and university campuses in the college guide section of a commercial bookstore. In addition, many states offer their own summer programs that are specifically geared to attract minority students.

A NOTE ON HOME SCHOOLING

In the past, home schooling was an obscure option that was reserved for people in rural settings or for religious conservatives. In recent years, however, this has become an option for people in the mainstream.

   When considering home schooling, certain things should be kept in mind about home schooling. To add to the integrity of home schooling, it's important to perform regular standardized testing to show progress and academic competency in particular areas, most notably in math, science, and reading. Most communities allow home schoolers to take these tests in the local public school. It's also a good idea that there be a number of teachers besides the primary parent-teacher. For example, if a few home-school families teamed together, certain parents could develop areas of specialty. That would add some diversity to the program.

Since home-schooled students study at home, student socialization is a concern. This problem can be dealt with by encouraging the student to get involved in sports or clubs at the local high school, church, or community agencies.

CONCLUSION

This brief introduction to high school choice should stimulate you to think more broadly about the possibilities that may be open to you. You shouldn't get hung up on trying to make "the" perfect choice. There are probably a few options that will serve you well. What I've detailed here is to get the discussion started for you and your family. If you get stuck, talk to your teachers and counselors at school. They're the best resources available to you.

I wish you the best of success as you begin high school! Above all else, enjoy the next few years of your young life!

Jacqueline V. McQueer
Phillips Academy, Andover, Massachusetts

Growing up in Cabrini Green Housing Projects in Chicago, Illinois, I was surrounded by broken hearts and shattered dreams. Generation after generation occupied these apartments where they lived and eventually died. The regular sounds of screaming and gun shots pierced the silence of our home as we slept. Black men dying, mamas crying, children playing, grandmas praying—the chaos never ended.

Giving honor to God, who is the head of my life, I would like to thank him for blessing me with the opportunity to attend Phillips Academy, a prep school in Andover, Massachusetts. Coming from the inner city of Chicago, I had never encountered so many people of different cultures and ethnic backgrounds. It was like an awakening. Asian, Indian, Caribbean, Dominican, and many other Americans as well as international students gathered together on the Phillips Academy campus to form a multicultural and diverse community. I entered the academy as a freshman in 1992 after graduating from Providence St. Mel, a private school in Chicago, with honors.

My expectations were high, and I was full of energy. I was accustomed to being at the head of the class, but I didn't realize that every student attending Phillips Academy had come from a school where they had also been at the head of their class. The competition was intense. Some students even felt that the only reason African-American and Latinos attended Phillips Academy was because the institution had to fill a certain percentage of the student body with minorities like myself. For years, I was troubled by this. Wanting to show them that I had as much right to attend this school as they did, I pushed myself. I pushed so hard to prove them wrong, I drove myself crazy. I almost gave up and threw my life away. It was because of faith, the love of my friends, my mother, and the faculty members at Phillips Academy that I gained enough strength and determination to continue my journey.

Now as a senior, I enjoy many tangible and intangible rewards owing to persistence and determination. I am currently the president of the Afro-Latino American Society, a varsity athlete, an assistant coach of one of our boys' basketball teams, a perfect R.A. in a freshman dorm, and a DJ on WPAA, our campus radio station. Through these activities, I have gained confidence and stamina. The social and educational values I accomplished at Andover will last a lifetime. My advice to students pursuing academic excellence is never give up because the best is yet to come. If you're going to play, play to win! Have no mercy and take no prisoners!

CHAPTER 2

Planning for the Future: Choosing the Right Field of Study, Faculty, and Counselor

RUBY C. DELERY

Associate Director of Admissions, University of Redlands, Redlands, California

> We are training not isolated [People], but a living group of [People]—nay, a group within a group. The final product of our training must be neither a psychologist nor a brick mason, but a person.
>
> —W. E. B. Du Bois, *The Souls of Black Folk*

"You can be anything you want to be in life" is a familiar phrase. How many times have you heard it from your parents, grandparents, other relatives, counselors, teachers, or friends? You have heard these words at least once in your lifetime, I am sure. The essence of someone encouraging you with these words is powerful. These words give liberty to dream, permission to impact this world, and approval to reach tangible goals. However, these words of inspiration are only partially true. Let me explain. Yes, you can be anything you want to be—a doctor, a marine biologist, a graphic artist, a lawyer, a teacher, a journalist—but preparation is the key to achieving these goals. Yes, you must prepare to become whatever you desire. I cannot begin to tell you how many students make quick decisions about what they want to be based on a remarkable absence of information. Students are unaware of basic academic preparation and the skills necessary to be successful in a particular area of study. Have you ever heard of people going to college, choosing a certain major, constantly changing their minds, and settling for whatever major is easiest and quickest in their opinion? It happens all of the time. Why set yourself up for disappointment? It isn't enough to choose a field of study based on glamour, salary, peer, or parent pressure. Choosing a field of study is an investment in your future, which means you should take deliberate steps to build a firm foundation that will ensure the best possible option for you. As you explore various fields of study, I urge you to keep a journal. Your journal will help you not only in keeping track of your progress, but also in monitoring and evaluating new developments and changes in your academic and personal interests. With the appropriate academic preparation, guidance, and an abundance of information, you can direct your field of choice.

The three components associated with preparing to choose a field of study are "soul-searching," academic preparation, and information gathering. What is soul-searching? It is getting down to the very elements that make up your personality. It is an honest assessment of your skills, which reinforces your strengths and cultivates your weaknesses. It is questioning your ability and adeptness. Assessing skills may be an uncomfortable feeling for some, but it is necessary to identify your strongest attributes. When asked to assess their skills, most students tend to emphasize their inadequacies and downplay their strengths. Some students even believe they do not have any skills because they are not yet adults. You do not have to be an adult to have skills, and nearly everyone has something they do well.

What are skills? Skills are developed aptitudes or abilities used every day that are gained through coursework, leisure activities, or work experience. They are not necessarily things you like to do or things you are interested in doing. Sometimes they are obvious, and sometimes they are not. For example, carrying out trigonometric functions involving sines, tangents, or cosecants may be "old hat," but the thought process involved in their execution is not. Skills are those things that are part of us, like communicating, thinking, reasoning, risk-taking, or time management. Have you thought about your skills? Answer the following questions using adjectives to describe your skills: What are my strengths? What are my weaknesses? What can I do to enhance my strengths and eliminate or reduce my weaknesses?

Once you have explored your skills, you must evaluate your academic foundation. Believe it or not, a correlation exists between subject areas you excel in and those you are interested in. You do well and succeed in the things that you enjoy and are good at. A strong academic foundation complements your selected field of study and is perhaps one of the most critical aspects of choosing a field of study. If you are academically prepared, you will have many options to choose from in college. Your study habits and the type of courses you select will have a direct impact on your readiness to pursue challenging courses in college. Your academic courses should be competitive and your grade point average solid. Your scholastic record should include college preparatory, honors, advanced placement, or International Baccalaureate courses such as English, intermediate algebra, U.S. history, biology, computer science, foreign languages, and literature. Elective courses such as typing, wood shop, auto mechanics, home economics, and the yearbook are not considered relevant courses for an academic field of study and should be kept to a minimum. I do not mean to suggest that these courses are not worthwhile. They do indeed have their place, but they are generally not seen as advantageous when you are seeking college entrance. If you want to be a doctor, for example, you must be on a college preparatory track in science. If you do not like or do well in biology, you might want to rethink that career choice.

Answer the following questions honestly. Am I taking college preparatory courses? How well am I doing in each course? Which subjects do I need to improve on? Keep in mind that the subject areas you enjoy, the skills you possess, and the dreams you have of "becoming" all belong to you.

To begin your search of possible fields of study, you must determine which area of examination is suitable for you. You can (1) examine the career or careers you are interested in pursuing and determine which field of study is best or (2) decide which fields you would like to study in college and which careers are associated with those particular areas. It does not matter how you choose to do your investigation as long as you explore a variety of possibilities. However, I urge you to keep the scope of your field of study broad. Take into consideration areas that will give you options and allow you to take full advantage of your academic, social, and interpersonal skills. As you develop and mature, new curiosities and concepts are certain to evolve. Therefore, all possibilities are viable, and there are no right or wrong fields of study. The more you know about the field(s) you are interested in, the better you will be able to make an informed decision about what is a good match for you.

There are many methods of gathering information about a particular field of study. One method is to utilize the guidance of faculty members or conduct informational interviews with professionals. These informal interviews can be extremely beneficial, for professionals in their various fields can offer insightful information about the career you may be interested in. These are but a few suggestions you can use as guidelines.

Sometimes students do not know how to get started on choosing a field of study. Well, you have two of the best resources you could possibly ask for: a faculty member and a counselor at your school. Believe it or not, faculty members and counselors want to help students reach their goals. They are great sounding boards who are, for the most part, willing to take the time to direct students to available information. Counselors and faculty members can provide you with or direct you to pertinent information on various fields of study. More importantly, they can give you a personal account of how they chose their field of study. All you have to do is be willing to let your aspirations be known. Ask for help.

The college/career center is perhaps one of the most under-utilized facilities on most high school campuses. The college/career center is filled with an immense amount of information. I am sure the counselors or staff in the center would appreciate your stopping by to capitalize on their services. If you are a student who is unfamiliar with the college/career center, I encourage you to make a conscious decision to explore it. The college/career center is an invaluable source of information ranging from computer software, such as Choices, Sigi Plus, and Guidance Information System (GIS), which analyze college majors and careers related to your skills, to references on colleges, financial aid, occupations, career trends, internships, and school visits from college representatives. Indeed, it offers a great deal of information on investigating field or college choices.

Another method is to conduct an informational interview with a professional person in an occupation about which you would like to know more. By conducting an informational interview, you will have an opportunity to obtain ideas on how to map out the process of getting to where you want to go. For example, interviewing someone in the field of accounting will give you first-hand knowledge of the field. It will offer you the chance to ask specific questions that are related to high school course preparation, college majors, internships, required exams, and perhaps graduate school. The information gathered at the interview will give you an up-close look at the final outcome.

Students should also keep in mind that college is not for everyone. Although college is an excellent place to get many social and academic experiences, it is also important to realize it is not necessarily required to be successful. In most cases, however, college will provide you with many more opportunities than a person who does not attend a college or university. The majority of upper-end jobs require a college education, and employers see the value of having employees who had the desire and skills to succeed in college. Keep this consideration in mind when exploring opportunities available upon your successful graduation from high school.

Choosing the right field of study is all about assessing your skills, academic strengths, and possibilities for the future. It is making a conscious effort to obtain as many choices as possible. As you begin to choose a field of study, continue to explore your dreams, goals, and aspirations. Do not be afraid to ask those around you for guidance. Utilize their knowledge for your benefit. Keep in mind that your first choice may not be your last. Students often change their major and interests several times. While this is not necessarily a bad thing, one should try to stay focused and make sure that all preparation will yield some positive results and experiences. The bottom line is that you should not be hasty in choosing a field of study just because it may yield grandeur. Rather, you should choose a field of study because you have explored all of the possibilities that will give you the opportunity to be anything you want to be in life. Remember, anything you choose to do or become is honorable. Everyone has the skills to become whatever they want, and you should strive to achieve your greatest potential and become a contributing member of society.

Berangere B. Robertson
University of Redlands, Redlands, California

"Your attitude will determine your altitude" is an inspirational message that my father often quoted me; it has become my motto and one of the keys to my success throughout my academic career. I was fortunate enough to be born into a highly educated family where learning both inside and outside the classroom was as natural as walking and breathing. In addition, I was taught that my blackness was not to be worn as a garment or a chip on my shoulder, but rather was the essence of my being and should always epitomize excellence. While enjoying my Afro-Caribbean heritage, I remained open to other cultures and creative ideas, which gave me the breadth and exposure necessary to be in sync with the world.

I was a very motivated and precocious adolescent and realized as early as junior high that I needed to assess my personal skills and take advantage of all the academic and social opportunities available to me. I knew that a positive attitude was important to the development of my personality and character, and that in assessing my skills, both my strengths and weaknesses were essential components of knowing myself and my dreams. Having grown up in a milieu where multiple languages and education were the norm, I accessed the opportunity to study other languages (Spanish and French) as well as extra math and science. This was done not only to broaden my cultural horizon, but also to enhance my opportunities in whatever field I would finally choose to pursue.

Upon entering high school, I felt that I had already prepared myself well academically, and so I wanted to continue my intellectual growth as well as balance my experiences with various extracurricular activities. I knew that government and history were not only my strongest subjects, but were also the fields that most gratified and stimulated my curiosity and my intelligence. However, my dedication and love for these subjects did not impede my striving to maintain good grades and even excel in other subjects such as math and science. I was constantly aware that a good GPA and high SAT scores coupled with extra-curricular activities, both social and community oriented, would be my passport to the premier institutions of higher learning. I believe that my keys to success have been dis-cipline, consistency, and self-determination. In knowing that I am not at my best when I must operate in an unor-ganized manner, I have always tried to be well prepared for my classes and exams. This is essential to my feeling confident about myself and the tasks that lie ahead.

In truth, while continually soul-searching, I found high school to be just an appetizer for the more challenging ex-periences of university academics and social life. Through college preparatory courses, my desire for college became so overwhelming that I overloaded on courses and gradu-ated a year earlier than my classmates. Yet this did not hinder me from participating in varsity sports or enjoying social activities with my fellow colleagues and church friends. I was quite fortunate in that I had few obstacles to overcome in high school except for my overwhelming de-sire to graduate early. Therefore, with the support of my family and friends coupled with initiative and determina-tion, I was able to accomplish that goal. I feel greatly blessed that I had motivated and supportive parents, as well as two older sisters who served as positive role models in their various academic endeavors. Their success, advice, and guidance only helped to influence and direct me in choosing the right path for my life.

I am deeply concerned and optimistic that my African-American brothers and sisters take advantage of every op-portunity to excel in whatever field they choose to bring them fulfillment. While the well-known cliché, "You can be anything you want to be in life," is true, you cannot fulfill your dreams overnight. Choosing a field of study and being successful is a process that requires preparing yourself, knowing your inner self, setting personal goals, and taking the initiative. Many resources are available to students, so tap in to them and begin to pave your own path to wherever it may lead you. In a highly technical and competitive society, a good education is still the most powerful and essential tool that one has to build the future.

CHAPTER 3

The Politics of High School

WILLIAM J. EKELER

Former Director of Student Leadership Activities, Radcliffe College,
Harvard University

Things are not always what they appear to be. With this in
mind, you should be aware of the politics of high school when
planning for a successful high school career. Since politics can
be both positive and negative, it is important that you recognize that they are present in many areas of life. An unending
number of possibilities could involve politics during your high
school years. Depending on where you attend high school and
the specific individuals involved with your high school experience, you as a black student will certainly encounter interesting dynamics. By recognizing that politics are most generally
present in many, if not all, aspects of your life (whether or not
they are intentional is entirely another matter), you will increase your opportunities for success in high school by learning
to deal with politics in an effective manner.

Before we look at specific dimensions of the political situation in the high school setting, we must first understand what the word "politics" means. Politics refers to an organized structure that is set in place by a particular board or set of lawmakers, usually a government. In a school situation the school board, administrators as well as faculty and staff, compose this body. These persons are responsible for conducting the business activities, writing/choosing the curriculum, and creating a safe and positive learning environment. All students, regardless of race, are required to comply with the guidelines established by the school system.

This brings us to the meaning and understanding of politics. Politics in the case of a high school refers to the dynamics that exist among the school board, administrators, faculty, staff, business community, parents, and you the student. These dynamics more specifically include the relationships and decision-making process involving all individuals who have the authority to make decisions and create the guidelines that students must ultimately follow. For example, if a faculty member has a strong belief that new computers need to be purchased for his school, and the administration and others disagree, a political situation will develop. The faculty may see an educational need for this technology, whereas the administration may feel it cannot supply the needed funds. The politics begin when interests from both sides are raised, usually discussed, and hopefully end with a decision rendered. Politics are often very shrewd, and people usually make compromises in order to achieve some of their strongest goals.

In high school many factors may involve politics. Let us first consider race and how it may be involved with politics. In the ideal, professionals act professionally and therefore race is not an issue in the classroom. Race is an important part of an individual's life, however, and depending on your situation, blacks may be treated in a number of ways. Unfortunately, some people view race as a descriptive characteristic and may stereotype a person's ability based on this view. As any level-headed person knows, individuals from all races across the world possess the ability to be successful. Those who choose to prove a political point or a personal theory, however, may cause race to be seen in a negative light. Those students who are in a position to interact with various races have a unique opportunity to learn about other cultures, traditions, and beliefs. If you have this opportunity, make it worth your while. Share your experiences and establish relationships with others who will enhance your knowledge and opportunity for success.

Gender can also present some interesting dynamics. Teachers may feel that certain courses or activities are better suited for male or female students. Therefore, you should work hard to become involved in any activities or classes that interest you. Some may try to discourage you from participation in areas that have typically been gender specific. However, keep in mind that it can be extremely beneficial to be the only one or one of a small number of individuals in a course or activity comprised mainly of the opposite sex. You can learn many lessons in such settings, including leadership qualities, group behavior patterns, group hierarchy, and basic interaction skills that will become routine in your professional life. Take advantage of the situation that allows you to interact with students of the opposite sex and use it as a learning experience.

Past experience can also be manipulated into a political situation in high school. Many of you could provide examples of students who have to live up to certain expectations. In many cases, blacks are automatically viewed as exceptional athletes, which may or may not be the case. A sibling may have been an excellent athlete or a superior student, and teachers may assume that the brother or sister will possess the same qualities. Often these past experiences are not valid, and sometimes you may need to remind your teachers or other students of this fact. The important point here is that, regardless of the expectations, you must become successful and work hard at the things that interest you and facilitate your goals. Remember that past experience, be it positive or negative, is never an indication of your success in the future.

Attitude and attendance may also play an important political part in your time at high school. These two components, though not ordinarily political in nature, do have an impact on the relationship between you and your teacher. The better your attendance and attitude, the greater chance you will have of developing a positive relationship with your teacher. Politics are about relationships, and as discussed earlier, you build those relationships to benefit your ultimate goals. Success in high school involves achievement in the classroom. One of the most effective ways to optimize your opportunities in the classroom is to have a positive relationship with your instructor. Your instructor will appreciate your good attendance and positive attitude and be more apt to assist you than if you did not possess these qualities.

Grading can also be extremely political. As we have discussed, those who hold positions of authority establish the parameters by which students operate. Some instructors count attendance as part of your grade. Other instructors may have a set grading pattern that results in a certain number of A's, B's, C's, D's, or even F's. You must therefore educate yourself as to your instructor's expectations and be sure that you fully understand his or her requirements. This understanding will allow you to "play" your political cards and work to achieve the goals you set for yourself.

Grades are also very important in future endeavors. For instance, when working towards admission to college or to secure employment, grades are a vital component. Some schools have admission or scholarship policies that might be seen as political. Although straight A's are not a written requirement for admission or scholarships at most institutions, they can be very influential in the decision-making process. While grades are not everything, you should strive to secure the highest grade point average possible.

As a black high school student, you will face your share of situations that involve politics. In order to achieve the highest degree of success possible, you must learn to deal effectively with issues and situations that involve politics. You must remember that just as adults have interests and ideas about how to fulfill those interests, you too have the right and responsibility to voice your opinions and concerns. Dealing with politics is frequently not easy and requires rational, intelligent thinking. Staying focused and informed and choosing your battles will serve you well.

Staying focused includes devising a plan, clearly communicating it, and following it through to achieve your desired results. Your plan is often just that and may need to be altered a great deal. If this happens, do not become flustered, for this is a common occurrence. Planning is important, but being able to revise your plan and rethink it often separates successful efforts from those that are not. Remaining focused and clear will allow others to better understand your ideas and will offer you a better opportunity for success.

Having good information that supports your plan is crucial. A person will frequently have great ideas and plans but no facts to support them. Whenever it is possible to support your theory or plans with facts, it is imperative that you do so. Ironically, a high school administrator once gave me that advice, and it has served me extremely well over the years. Individuals who disagree with your ideas or simply do not like them will inevitably challenge them. The best defense for your ideas is a well-founded, substantiated offense. What this means is that you have facts, examples, and information that greatly support or prove your theory. With this information you will have greatly increased your opportunity for a successful effort.

Finally, choose your battles and do not expect that things will always go your way. Choosing your battles means that you will not always prevail, and thus you must decide what issues are most important to you and prepare relentlessly to achieve your objectives. Your peers and adults will respect you more if you work well with others to achieve results and prepare even more diligently to accomplish goals that are most important to you.

In closing, keep in mind that politics will be present during your high school years. In order to keep politics positive and to have them work to your advantage, you must remain focused, be informed, choose your battles wisely, and realize that things may not always go as planned. Recognizing that politics exist in high school is only the first step in making the most of your high school years. Approaching the political structure of your given situation with tact and an understanding that you must operate within its parameters will allow you to obtain the highest degree of success possible.

Demond L. Finister
University of Nebraska, Lincoln

My home economics teacher, Sadie White, told me once that I was a very special kind of kid who would make a difference in my life and the lives of others. She said, "You're at rock bottom, and the only way for you is up. You just have to keep your head up and believe in yourself."

She was right, I would make a difference in my life and the lives of others. I have a nine-year-old baby brother named Lennis who thinks I'm the smartest person in the world. He tells me that he wants to be just like me; yet, I want to be just like him. He does not know the complete story behind my success.

Ever since the first grade, I have had problems getting along in school. My mother told me that it was a learning disability. I had to study all day to comprehend things like subtracting (I had to use my fingers) and trying to read words like *cat, at, that,* and *hat.* My brothers would maybe spend thirty minutes studying, and when report card time came around, they would race home to show off their A's and B's. I would walk in the house much later with tears flooding my eyes, because I had nothing more to show than F's. I cried because my brothers would tease me on the way home. I would also be hurt because my mom could only hug me for trying, and I knew she did not blame me. In spite of this, I would look up at my mother and tell her, "I promise I'll get good grades the next time," but the results were always the same. It was not until I was a sophomore at Jesuit High School that my luck changed.

At first, I felt that Jesuit was an overwhelming high school. It had four big buildings, the majority of the students were white Americans, and the courses were twice as hard as any I had ever taken before. For years I lived right across the street from the high school, but it had never crossed my mind that I might want to attend. Then one day when I was walking home from school, the head coach of the football team saw me and called out, "Hey, can I talk to you for a second?" I still remember that he asked me what my time was in the forty-yard dash. I told him 4.4. He looked at me for a long time with what appeared to be a gleam in his eyes. Then he asked me if I wanted to play football for the Jesuit Blue Jays. There was no way I was going to refuse his offer after I looked at the size of the school.

Two months after I began attending Jesuit, I was on the verge of being kicked out because of my grades. Two weeks before the playoffs, I was off the team. I was seventeen years old, two years behind my grade, and I could not understand why this was happening to me. I tried to keep my head up, but I just couldn't do it anymore. Suicide continued to cross my mind, and finally I decided that I did not want to deal with the pain anymore. My counselor talked me out of doing it, and for the rest of that day we talked about my problems at home and school. I told him about my learning disability and my constant struggle to pass to the next grade. In closing our conversation, he told me that I could no longer attend Jesuit, but he gave me a card that had the name of a man who would help to make me the person I am today, Father Bob Allanach.

I was desperate for help, so I called him and explained my situation. He dropped everything he was doing and came right over to my house to talk. He told me the first step in getting help was to find it. For some unexplainable reason, I began to feel good about myself, and I saw a light starting to shine on me. Father Bob decided that I needed a fresh start somewhere. I thought he was talking about a school that was not as hard as Jesuit. I did not think he meant relocating me three states away from Louisiana. My first reaction was that I would rather work at a local grocery store for the rest of my life than go to another state without any friends or family. But I reminded myself about all of the turmoil and depression that I had gone through and how bitter I was. I knew that this was my chance to make a comeback. Father told me more about this place, and I started to become excited about going. He said that I could have anything I wanted. He told me that I would have someone helping me with my studies every day and that it snowed there most of the year. That was all I needed to know to convince myself that I really did want to go. For the next two and a half years, I would spend my time reconstructing my life, learning to read, and receiving my high school diploma. Most of all, I was making my mom proud of my report cards and other academic achievements at a place called Boys Town in Omaha, Nebraska.

The day I graduated from Boys Town was the happiest day of my life and one of the happiest days for my mother. In spite of all the heartache I had to endure—a learning disability, being teased by my brothers, getting kicked out of school because I could not handle the academics, thinking of committing suicide, and living away from home for two and a half years—I still found a way to overcome adversity. I never want to go back into the "hole" again. I found that I could achieve success in spite of problems I encountered. I just needed to find the help so I could help myself!

CHAPTER 4

Opportunities for Success in the Classroom

SHANNON D. MATHEWS

Admissions Counselor, Pomona College, Claremont, California

Success in the classroom can be seen in many ways. The most common type of this success comes from receiving an A on a classroom activity. Although grades are one of the easiest measurements of success available to you, they are not the only way to determine academic excellence. Receiving the highest grade possible is indeed desirable, but realize that other opportunities for success do exist. A student's academic performance can be viewed in numerous ways. Consider the student who does not receive an A but who improves his performance from a C to a B. This, too, is an achievement, marking academic success and reflecting the student's desire to continuously work toward improvement. Your academic success today is not necessarily indicative of your success in the future. Working to improve shows others that you have not given up on yourself, so others will not likely give up on you. Persistence is a valuable trait, and chances are that others will likely help you to obtain your goals.

Another type of success in the classroom, and one that is much easier to accomplish, is classroom behavior. How you act in class is just as strong a determinant of your future success in high school as getting the highest grade possible. Good classroom behavior will prove especially beneficial when you need job or academic recommendations. Not surprisingly, teachers generally write better recommendations for students who behave responsibly in the classroom.

Good classroom behavior does not mean that you have to be "teacher's pet" or "kiss up." Rather, it means understanding classroom rules and choosing to follow them or even turning in class assignments on time. Handing in your assignments when they are due is an excellent way for you to demonstrate to your teachers that you respect their time and that you value your education. It also gives your teachers enough time to grade your assignments and to keep to their planned schedules for the class. In addition, teachers will likely be less critical about an assignment that is turned in on time. This will not automatically earn you a higher grade, but it will guarantee your ability to earn the highest grade possible. So by exhibiting good behavior in your work habits, you help yourself and your teachers.

Another factor of good behavior in the classroom is involvement or your in-class contributions. The most basic form of this behavior is raising your hand in class. Do not be afraid to volunteer your efforts in class because each time you do so you have a new opportunity to succeed. For example, if a student raises her hand and answers a question incorrectly, she lets the teacher know that she wants to be an active participant in learning. Shortly after, she will undoubtedly find out the correct answer, thus, ultimately adding to her knowledge. If the same student raises her hand and answers a question correctly, she continues to let the instructor know that she is serious about her education, and she has most likely added to the level of respect the instructor has for her. Also, answering a question correctly or contributing your opinions in class helps those around you add to their level of knowledge. In classes where participation is part of your grade, this can be a simple way to achieve a better grade. Although it may be harder for some, how hard is it to raise your hand anyway? If you are reticent or shy, remember that everyone in the class has a right to contribute their ideas.

The more you contribute in class, the more those around you will have an opportunity to get to know you a little bit better. In this way, they are more likely to respect what you bring to the classroom. This allows you to have a better relationship not only with your peers, but with your teachers as well. As a result, you develop relationships with the people who can give you the support you may need to succeed in a particular class. For example, if your peers respect you more, they may be more open to forming a study group that may be just the help you need to succeed with your homework. Your instructor may even be willing to stay after school to assist you with the subjects that are most difficult for you.

It is critical that if you do not understand something, be it as small as a single word or as large as a complex theory, you must seek out the answer. Asking for assistance is not admitting failure, but is simply showing the desire to want to learn. Make sure that you ask for explanations just as soon as you start to get confused. It is important to do so right away because many things you learn may be based on principles that must be understood one at a time.

Keep in mind that you cannot succeed in the areas of performance and behavior if you are not in class. Therefore, constant classroom attendance is crucial. Those who choose not to attend classes everyday completely terminate some of their opportunities for success through performance, behavior, and involvement.

One of your most crucial investments in your future starts with simply showing up to class. The student who genuinely cares about his or her future dreams and goals will also care enough to invest in his education by not wasting time. If your attendance has been down in the past, you should work on improving it; if it has always been up, then maintain that effort.

When you attend class everyday, you decrease the chance you will miss something important, which in turn increases your chances to expand your understanding of a subject. The more information you are exposed to in class, the better your chances will be to achieve the academic performance you desire. It is also a good way to ensure that you will be able to spot your weaker areas at an earlier stage. If you understand where you need to improve, you can get help from the instructor or your peers long before any dreaded exam. You increase the likelihood of success in your classes by just making the effort to show up for those classes.

Showing up on time is also important, for it shows true respect for the opportunity you have to be educated. Although many of us view education as an expectation, it is still a privilege that even others in our community did not or may not have. Being on time will also add to how your instructors view you and can lead to a healthy relationship with them and strengthen the notion that you probably have been around to hear all of the things your instructor has said in class.

The best way to learn is to get information for yourself. If a student thinks he can get information from someone else or borrow notes and it will be the same as being in class, he is sadly mistaken. Note taking is an individual skill that no two people do exactly the same way. For example, if your friend is taking notes and is not struggling in the same area that you are, he might not take lengthy notes in an area where you would have. In this situation, your friend's notes will cause you to miss out on some vital information that might have helped you understand the difficult points a little more clearly. Thus, you should never rely solely on another person's notes instead of first-hand exposure to a subject.

Let us look at another example. Suppose you miss class on Tuesday, and on that day the instructor reviews information that will be on an exam that Thursday. Although your friend tells you about the test, he forgets to tell you about one of the four sections it covers. You will likely be surprised by the omitted section and, as a result, you will probably not get the grade you wanted on that particular test. If you had been in class on Tuesday, this situation would have been drastically different. Missing class should therefore be a relatively rare occurrence, caused only by illness or some other unforeseen event.

Success in the classroom is all about making good choices: the choice to work hard, to care about what happens inside the classroom, and to be present. There is no one way to obtain success in the classroom, but we have discussed several ways that will allow us to tailor our choices for success. Indeed, your individual success in life is about choice: that of using every opportunity you are given wisely. As a result, remember that success in the classroom is something that you yourself make and is not simply given.

Tia Villeral
Redlands Senior High School, Redlands, California

My classroom success is largely the result of an improvement in my overall involvement. I was the typical high school student who never contributed my ideas in class, but instead just sought out the teacher after class. My history teacher began to encourage me to speak out in class. Although I can't say that I began to speak out in every class, I did decide to occasionally raise my hand. The more I added in class, the easier raising my hand became, and I began to gain confidence. My teacher noticed this confidence as well, and as a result she recommended me for an Advanced Placement history class. As many students know, an Advanced Placement class is not always the easiest experience, but I am fortunate that my teacher recommended me because now it will better my chances for college. I began to realize that raising my hand in class wasn't as hard as it used to be, and I know more of my teachers now than I would have being that shy, quiet freshman I used to be. I also realize that if it is easy now, then maybe it won't be so hard in college either.

Another factor contributing to my success in the classroom has been my attendance. When you are in honors or AP classes, it's very important to make sure you don't miss a lot of class periods because so much information is covered that lots of absences could really put you behind. These kinds of classes are supposed to be a challenge, but they are even more challenging if you miss a couple of days and you find yourself behind by several weeks. I must say that I do not always get excited about going to class and it isn't always easy to go, but I do, and when I am there I am a step ahead of the kid who isn't!

CHAPTER 5

Study Habits and Hints

MARGARET FLORENCE

Head Librarian, North High School, Des Moines, Iowa

By the grace of God you've made it to high school, one of your many dreams come true. In high school, you get to make choices, and one of the most important choices you will ever make there is whether to be popular or to be smart. Take charge of yourself at this very moment and decide on one of the two. Now that you are here, I want you to stay. I want you to leave with a diploma. You're "makin' it."

Up to this point in your schooling, you have been comfortable as part of "the group," but now the time has come for you to prepare for a future seriously. For some of you, high school will mean taking a risk, giving up some of your old friends, because they will be going in a different direction with their lives. You will probably change your way of doing things. Sometimes it will be lonely for those of you who have shown courage in deciding to be smart. "Makin' it" takes some personal focus. Remember, when *you* leave high school you will have a diploma, a ticket to your future.

You have everything to work with that the greats—Inhotep, Nzingha, Banneker, Marshall, and Carson—had: Brains, the ability to think! If these names are not familiar to you, then go to the library right now and find out their relationship to you. Learning about them will help you understand who you are and what you are and what you are capable of doing. Let them be your role models: They knew what they wanted, and they persevered until they achieved their goals. They had the power to imagine their goals; indeed, everyone has the power to imagine, even you.

To make the most of your high school education first, calm down emotionally. You are so excited about high school and all it offers. Second, develop some simple organizational and time management techniques. Third, establish the habit of being on time and prepared for class. Being prepared for class means having materials for the class: book, pen, and paper, as well as the lesson prepared. This will help reduce the stress associated with class schedules, homework, sports, extracurricular activities, and a job.

Were you ever taught how to study efficiently? Teachers often assume that you know how to study. You do not study in the same way for every subject; therefore, you will need to acquire a set of study skills that work for you. You may know some people who seem to be able to do more in less time and get good grades. Their trick is that they know how to study. You, too, can learn this trick. You also need to develop some habits—that is, customary practice or manners performed through frequent repetition until they are part of you.

Time management—what to do when—is the single most important skill to master. Learn to make a daily schedule in which you list study time and personal time (fun). Write your assignments, due dates, and test dates on a calendar. This will help you stick to your task and complete your assignments on time. Learning to manage your time is not a familiar skill, but it is one you can learn. Most of the other study skills you will develop are linked to the manipulation of time.

Next, decide where you are going to study. Home may not provide the best atmosphere for you. You should therefore seek out the school library, which is usually free of small children, the radio, the television, and the telephone. If you work a job (which many of you must) and carry a full schedule, you may need to look at the public library or make use of the study hall time to study. Study hall is not a "handout"; it means just that—a place to study. In order to study, sometimes you will need to be creative with your time management.

Learn to say "No" to that little voice that says "Let's Party" or "Go ahead and call; it won't take long," or "I'm too tired to do this." Learning to say "No" is an absolute necessity for academic success. Self-discipline or self-management is learned; it is not easy, but it can be learned.

Some of you may ask, Why study anyway? Because it is an organized way to achieve your goals. The more you know, the more you are prepared to do and the more you are ready when opportunity comes. You learn what you want to know—for example, rap songs: you watch a video, you practice dance moves, you listen carefully to the words (over and over). Those same skills—observation and practice—apply to your high school success. You must have that same zeal for your academic success.

While not every successful student studies in the same way, all of them study. Good study habits have more to do with a student's success or lack of success than interest in the subject. Students who study and review regularly can usually approach a test with 80 to 90 percent recall, compared to about 50 percent recall among students who study without regular review. If it is worth the time to do, do it right; aim for a top grade, not just to get it done.

One of the most important things about daring to be successful is your attitude. Do you want to learn? Are you afraid of the commitment to learn? Again it comes down to the question, Do you want to be popular or to be smart? Do you care about peer pressure? You have a right to read, write, spell, and compute; doing so is not "act'n white." When you get an "A" and make the honor roll, those are not "act'n white" skills, but the skills of the smart people who studied. If you are going to survive in an integrated society, you need to learn the system in order to take your rightful place within that society. You will need to be alert (listen); you will need to watch (observe); you will need to have study skills (methods); and most of all you will need to be self-disciplined (focused). It is always wise to participate in your class in some positive way because you should never let anyone get the idea that you are stupid. I use the term *stupid* rather than *ignorant* because stupid means you are dumb, while ignorant means you do not know. Do not, through your attitude, perpetuate the idea of being unable to learn.

Attitude is the way you communicate your mood to others and the way you see things mentally. It is your mind-set. The more you can focus on the positive factors of your environment, the easier it will be to stay positive.

All of us encounter events that can shake our attitude. Your challenge is to quickly adjust your attitude, allowing you to bounce back and regain your positive outlook. Your attitude is a priceless possession. Don't let anyone take that from you. We are what we believe ourselves to be. You can tell about yourself and never say a word.

Once you have mastered self and the use of time management, you are feeling good about yourself. Let's take a look at developing the habit of note taking. Do you realize you forget about 80 percent of what you hear within two weeks? So write it down—write down the instructor's main ideas; copy everything on the board; put down what you think you will need to remember. Taking notes will keep you alert in class, help you review, and prepare you for class participation. If your school offers a class in note taking, take that class. Also, be sure to attend class everyday; only you know what you need to record for your memory.

Develop your own shorthand for note taking. For example, abbreviate words (building, bldg); use common symbols (e.g., for example; c, about; and i.e., that is); underline key words. Certain teachers will give you hints on note taking in their subject, so listen and follow directions. These little hints keep you attentive and help you record what you need to know from a lecture. I suggest experimenting with a style (e.g., an outline) when writing notes from textbooks. You need to organize facts to show relationships. Write down every word of a rule, quote, or law. Write clearly in your own words in order to read and review your notes later; you will understand the material better when it is written in your own words. And oh yes—read!

Reading varies with the type of materials you are reading as well as the purpose for which you are reading. For example, you do not read science in the same manner that you read literature. To save time and remember more, learn to read more efficiently. If you are looking for general ideas, skim; if you want details, read slowly, carefully, and even aloud if necessary to attain a particular point of information. Hearing it may help memory. Increase your thinking skills by becoming a more critical reader. Question what you read. Yes, you do have to read and read and read. You must learn to apply special reading skills when you study complicated materials.

In this regard, I want to suggest the SQ3R formula for reading assignments:

Survey
Question
Read and underline
Recite and write
Review

Survey—10 minutes: An Overview

Examine the chapter title and introduction; then note the headings, subheadings, and bold words. Skim the chapter summary.

Glance at the diagrams, charts, and picture annotations. You have just previewed the chapter. Previewing makes understanding the chapter so much easier. You still have to read.

Question

Turn the headings into questions; use the question words *who, what, when, where,* or *how.* This gives purpose for reading. Your mind will automatically hone in on what you have previewed, which adds understanding and recall.

Read and Underline

Now you are ready to read and make notations (after you read). Make sure you understand the meaning of the words you read. You may not use these words when you talk, but you will need to understand them in order to get the full meaning of what you are reading and to communicate with others. I hope you have a dictionary.

Recite and Write

Recite the answers to the questions you formulated from the headings.

Review

Go over the notes and any questions or activities at the end of the chapter. Review the complete chapter.

At first, the SQ3R formula for reading will seem difficult and a lot of trouble. But remember that new processes are always hard to learn, so just keep trying until you learn how.

Don't be afraid to ask your instructor questions. Timing is everything in asking a question. Do you know the instructor's style well enough to interrupt? Get the instructor's attention by raising your hand. Face the person, head up, and politely ask your question; then thank the instructor for the explanation. If a class interruption is not possible, then, at the end of the class period ask for an appointment to discuss your question. There is usually not enough time before or after school unless you ask the instructor to make time for you. Be on time for your appointment and have your question written out to save time and to clarify your thinking before the meeting. Remember, the only dumb questions are the ones you don't ask.

During your time in high school, you will be required to do a lot of writing. Whenever you are faced with an information problem (or have to make a decision that is based on seeking information), you can use the following step-by-step problem-solving process. I use it everyday in the school setting, as well as the home setting.

I teach all my students the BIG SIX Information Problem-Solving Process from Michael Eisenberg and Robert Berkowitz's workshop, Information Problem Solving. It has proven to be an extremely useful tool when doing a research paper.

1. **Task Definition**
   What needs to be done?
   Write it down or verbalize it.

2. **Information-Seeking Strategies**
   What resources can you use?
   Can you name the possible resources available?

3. **Location and Access**
   Where can you find these resources?

4. **Use of Information**
   What can you use from these resources?
   Extract information from the resource.
   Take notes.

5. **Synthesis**

What can you do to finish the job?
How do you organize all the resources
you have found into one whole product?

6. **Evaluation**

How will you know you have done a good job?
Go back to step one and see if you have answered the
question to the best of your ability, get some feedback,
and check your draft.
Is the problem solved? Hand in a neat copy. You are
the judge.

We have not discussed taking a test. Taking a test enables
you to check your study habits and skills. Have you mastered
them? The test will show what you know. There are several
points to consider in a testing situation.

For an objective test:

- Your attitude—consider it something to outwit (contest).
- Survey the test quickly and get some perspective on the questions.
- Pay attention to qualifiers (usually, none, always).
- Write neatly.
- For multiple-choice questions, read all the answers before you choose. Eliminate the choices that are obviously wrong. Choose from what is left.

For an essay test:

- Read through the test.
- Note key words by underlining.
- Briefly outline (up in the corner of your test) the points you plan to cover.

- Use facts and examples to support your answers.
- Proofread your answers.

Carefully review your returned test; it will show you where your study skills are weak. Take criticism from the instructor and others so that you can learn. At the same time, you can help someone else because giving and sharing helps you, too, when you are studying.

What happens when you have managed your time, organized yourself and your work, and still get discouraged and bogged down? This will happen, but expect it! Look around you—have you done all you can for yourself? Is there a place to get tutoring help? Is there someone in your class who seems to understand and will help you? Can you talk to the instructor? Can the librarian help? Don't be afraid to ask for help. Don't wait until you are overwhelmed to seek help. In fact, as soon as you do not understand the material, seek help. You could organize your own study group. Studying together really is a good idea. Share ideas. Stick together with those who have the same interest.

You can dispel the myth of academic inferiority among African-American students. When you succeed, it's because of ability, effort, and courage to study and really "make it," not luck. Do not be ashamed of academic achievement. Understand you have a right to be smart. Show it. It is your choice. While grades are not always an accurate reflection of abilities and potential for success, they definitely impact both your career and college success. Go for it! Success is yours! It isn't over until you walk across the stage for that diploma.

Charles E. Stewart, Jr.
North High School, Des Moines, Iowa

High school is a very crucial time in everyone's life. Your success or failure in high school greatly affects the life you will live. I have found that success in high school is largely dependent on having a positive attitude, good discipline, and just plain old-fashioned studying.

Attitude is a little difference in people that makes a major difference in the outcome of their lives. A positive attitude is vital for success both in school and in life. With a good attitude, I have met academic disappointment with an inspiration to do better. It often seems that having a good attitude uplifts not only yourself and your teachers, but your peers also.

After much trial and error, I have learned that there is no substitute for studying. What makes a difference is how you study. Do you study for comprehension or for recitation? Do you study better in the mornings or in the evenings? I encourage all students to answer these questions for themselves. Afterward, they should modify their current study habits to make sure they are getting the most out of their time.

Discipline is a necessary foundation for success in high school. By discipline I mean taking the responsibility upon yourself to learn and to understand. It takes discipline to pay attention in class. By exercising discipline in my life, it becomes my responsibility to tell my friends that I have school work to do. Being able to say no, and setting off a special time for school, will often help you enjoy your social gatherings much more.

Effective study habits, a positive attitude, and self-discipline have helped me to achieve success not only in academics, but also in other social endeavors. My final advice to high school students is to have fun; but remember that you only go through high school once, so make the most of it.

CHAPTER 6

Athletics

WILLIE HILL

Head Track and Field Coach, Morehouse College, Atlanta, Georgia

Large numbers of high school young people are interested in or currently participating in athletics. Athletic participation gives students a sense of pride that comes from displaying their abilities in a controlled environment. In addition, successful athletic participation provides a conduit to higher education through the scholarship process. For a very few athletes, this same participation provides them with opportunities for a more intense experience in the professional arena.

We often hear the term *student athlete* to describe a currently enrolled student who is participating in authorized sports activities. That term is significant because it touches on an important concept. In high school, you can't have the athlete part without the student.

Student athletes are a special breed of people who have two major responsibilities. First, they must be intellectually capable of mastering the academic, cognitive component of their educational enhancement. Second, they must also be tenacious enough and committed to overcoming the rigors of athletic participation. This conjoined term would seem initially to comprise two directly opposing concepts. This is a major misconception. These concepts should be understood to complement and support each other rather than to be in conflict.

When athletes believe that they cannot or do not have to participate effectively and successfully in class, they are shortchanging themselves and are buying into the stereotype. In order to be an athlete and to exercise the available options, you must be willing to sacrifice even more. The student athlete who is both academically and athletically solid is a wonderful addition to a team. This student has emphasized discipline in his or her life. Such a person is a coach's dream.

One of the age-old questions student athletes ask is, "How much time should a student athlete spend studying or practicing to be a top athlete?" The combination of intellect and athletic prowess is not a new phenomenon peculiar to the twentieth century. Persons of African heritage have always been both intellectually and athletically competent. Each student athlete must determine how much time is required and must set aside the time required to achieve excellence in both endeavors. If you are good in track and football but are having some difficulty with Spanish or chemistry, you know that you need to devote extra time for the development of skills and competencies in your subject. Both your coach and teacher want equal output from you. The answer to the question above, therefore, is: whatever amount of time the individual knows is required for excellence.

High school athletics can be extremely competitive. Some schools have longstanding traditions of championships in certain sports. Each of you can probably identify schools in your town, city, or state that have consistently had championship teams in football, basketball, track and field, baseball, volleyball, and so on. Coaches and athletes have dedicated themselves to excellence and are willing to stay the course. Since studying and class participation are keys to academic success, practice and more practice are the keys to athletic success. Coaches, in many instances, may be teachers. This means that you may have to pull double duty for one person, and more will be required from you.

A leader in the simplest definition is an individual who helps the group accomplish its goal by identifying how it is to be done and motivating others to help. In this sense, all athletes—not just the team captains and co-captains—are viewed as leaders. Student athletic leadership is important not only to the coach but also to the student. Once you have taken a leadership role, you are more likely to have confidence to do it again. Coaches are very supportive of calculated risk-takers—those athletes who are willing to step out to make the big important plays but are skilled and confident enough to expect success from their actions. For example, it is the last few seconds of a championship basketball game; should the team members pass to the player who has a record of making 89 percent of his or her outside shots or should the shot go to a player who has a record of 55 percent? We know that each has a 50 percent chance of making the shot, but the risk is impacted by the one who has a greater probability of success. Does the track coach put the slowest runner on the last leg of the relay team?

Both male and female athletes are excelling in a variety of sports at the high school level. African-American students are expanding their options through participation in a wider variety of sports. Traditionally, blacks have excelled in football, basketball, track, baseball, and volleyball. Today the options have increased, and you will find students involved in wrestling, softball, field and ice hockey, soccer, swimming, gymnastics, tennis, golf, rugby, and so on. High school student athletes need these options. Just as academic options offer some variety for the student, options should be available in the realm of sports.

Female athletes are now taking advantage of all available sports options. African-American female athletes have not always had variety in their options, once being limited basically to basketball, track and field, volleyball, and softball. Now the menu has more selections, and larger numbers of female athletes are participating. Because of past practices, young women have relatively few female athlete role models, including Althea Gibson, Cheryl Miller, Alice Coachman, and Wilma Rudolph. Role models, however, do not have to be exactly like you. You can pull from the characteristics of a Michael Jordan, Edwin Moses, Emmitt Smith, Tiger Woods, and Arthur Ashe. You can reach for the best and identify what you can use to set goals for yourself. In this endeavor, you should reach back into history. Who were some of the African-American female sports pioneers? Conduct research on the sport that especially interests you and identify its pioneers and champions.

Expanding the involvement of student athletes is important. Specifically, the student athlete should be involved not just in school activities but also in the community. Numerous civic, social, and religious organizations in your community are looking for young people to assist them in providing services to others. You are probably thinking that you don't have time to devote to anything else. But remember that community involvement is important in being a well-rounded person; it is also important in developing skills among contributing members of society. How many of you participated in Little Leagues? How many of you received some type of help from a civic club, fraternity, or sorority? How many of you found satisfaction through participation in activities sponsored by your church? Involvement may take some of your time, but the rewards you receive from those you help will more than compensate for your time. In addition, colleges and universities have begun to require co-curricular activities for its students. You might as well get in some early experience so that you can be ahead of the game.

Dreams are important to all young people, including student athletes. A dream should serve as a prelude to a plan, and a plan should contain real steps required to make a dream come true. What is your dream? Young student athletes must be realistic and honest about their skills and abilities. Some may be dreaming of becoming a coach and providing the same experiences for others that they have had. Others may dream of becoming an entertainer, educator, judge, or doctor. Still others may dream of becoming a professional athlete. Do you have what it takes to make your dream a reality? When you make your plans, be sure that you allow for options. Don't plan to be a doctor if your skills and interests in science and math subjects are deficient. The high school athlete usually dreams of becoming the consummate professional athlete, making the big bucks and driving the fancy cars. Is this a realistic dream for you? The percentage of new people entering the ranks of the professional athlete each year is limited. Begin to compare yourself to those who are currently in the professional sports arenas. Do you have what it takes to compete with them? Will you have what it takes in a few years? Remember, you will have a more difficult group of contenders because athletes are always improving. Your dream and plan must be grounded in fact, not fantasy.

Success and failure are always out there. How do you reach or maintain your success level and reduce your failure rate? High school student athletes must have what it takes to be successful. Consider some of the following characteristics as you conduct a self-assessment in an effort to continue the quest for success. How many fit you? For success, you should be

self-motivated	a calculated risk-taker
a self-starter	an energetic participant
intelligent	a planner
persistent	decisive
determined	a realist
honest	hard working

Success breeds success. The more successful you are, the more you build confidence and self-esteem.

The old African proverb that it takes a village to raise a child should be considered relevant today. Growing up in our cities and towns is not an easy task to accomplish, and every day we see evidence of some people not making it out. Parents need to be an important part of your lives, supporting and protecting you. They are much wiser than you think. Some of you have opted for the extended family model, seeking the company and counsel of others who are not directly related to you. You have expanded your family to include people you now call your second mother or father, or possibly your aunt and uncle. You may also have added a few older sisters and brothers because you needed some more relationships. Try to listen to the wisdom of the elders. You must, however, be able to think for yourself.

Being a student athlete is very rewarding. Combining the academic and athletic sides of your life can be done and be done very well. There is no secret formula that someone can give you, because you must devise your own formula. You are the main player in this game; you are the one who must break the tape at the end of the mile. Athletics presents a wonderful arena of activities, but it is not an easy ride. Indeed, those who succeed in being student athletes have a greater chance of being successful in life.

Sheba Rugege
Grambling State University, Grambling, Louisiana

Young, gifted, and black is what we are. We are the descendants of kings and queens, the products of over 400 years of struggle for freedom and justice, and the essential key to the advancement of our great race. We have the responsibility of following many challenging models: the undying spirit of Malcolm X, the courage of Harriet Tubman, the humility of Dr. Martin Luther King, Jr., and the exceptional bravery of Nelson Mandela. Frederick Douglass once said, "If there is no struggle, there is no progress." Many struggled so that we could be where we are today. As Emile Cabral used to say, "alute continua"—the struggle continues; now we must make progress. Our ancestors toiled and persevered through the vicious faces of racism and injustice, and we can only put forth our absolute effort to ensure that their sacrifices were not in vain.

How can we succeed as young African-American high school students? Presently, I am a sophomore at Grambling State University, but I would have never made it here without the struggle, love, and discipline of many. Though we live in an age in which prayer has been taken out of the schools, we must put God first. If a spiritual being is not present in one's life, there is no reason why a child should find anything wrong with alcohol, sex, or even murder. A strong, stable, supportive, and loving family background is vital to one's moral standing and outlook on the future. Proverbs 22:6 reads, "Train up the child in the way he should go and when he is old, he will not depart from it." If a child is raised to think that education is the passport to a successful future, and the thought is constantly repeated, he will not stray. My parents always instilled in me the fact that a C was never good enough. They told me that a C is average, and I was certainly not average. Our long dreams and ambitions will come true only when we understand that we cannot settle for less: We must always shoot for the stars.

Since the civil rights era, African Americans have found comfort in the few rights and privileges we have been granted. Although we have several African-American mayors, thousands of prominent national leaders, and an end to Jim Crow, an ex-Klansman was almost elected to the office of governor in Louisiana; affirmative action is being terminated; and many "Mark Furmans" are still patrolling our city streets. "He who starts behind in the great race of life must forever remain behind or run faster than the man in front," said Dr. Benjamin E. Mays. This scholar is telling us that we must always be two steps ahead to succeed in this country.

Another step to success is finding some sort of inspirational and motivational person or group in your life, whether it is a teacher, a counselor, an upperclassman, a community organization, or just a friend. The Husia states that "The friend of a fool is a fool. The friend of a wise person is another wise person." When you surround yourself with positive forces, you will begin to speak, dream, and live positively.

You owe yourself nothing but the BEST. Strive hard so that one day you will be someone that the next generation will read about in their African-American history books. Those people were no more special than you! All of you were made in God's likeness, and God does not make mistakes, so you are here for a reason. One of the biggest fears people have is the fear of success. Don't let that stop you from shining like the star that you are. Remember, you came from kings and queens who have ruled before, so take back your throne and reign once more.

CHAPTER 7

Extracurricular Activities

HOLLY A. ROBERTSON

Admissions Counselor, Pennsylvania State University, University
Station, Pennsylvania

SOCIAL INTERACTIONS

As a preschool and primary school-aged child, I was socialized
to have positive interactions with others. I would interact with
neighborhood playmates and other children, usually when our
parents got together. I lived in a neighborhood that housed a
community/recreation center that provided structured programs and allowed unstructured social activities after school,
on weekends, and throughout the summer. During the school
year there were always school and community-sponsored functions. At times certain students were selected for participation
in special events, and other times it was up to the individual
(perhaps with some encouragement) to participate on his own.
I was fortunate to have parents who encouraged me and allowed me to explore just about any interest I had. Some inter-

ests were short lived, but I at least had several opportunities to do some very special things.

The elementary and junior high/middle school years are the prime years for young people to develop strong interaction skills and, better yet, natural leadership talents. Think of those individuals who were regularly selected to be team captains, called on frequently to answer questions, or asked to come up to the front of the line (line leader). Through social interactions, these students were being groomed to represent their peers, schools, communities, or families. Socialization became important not only because these individuals were good or had the potential to be great people, but also because an investment had been made to develop them socially by involving them in a variety of interactions to showcase their talents.

Involvement

Extracurricular activities provide crucial opportunities for young people to get involved in their schools, communities, social groups, athletics, and political action. With appropriate stimulation or natural instinctive desire, individuals will show interest in particular activities, frequently through neighborhood/community groups, family interests, or school functions. Adults can help young people realize their natural talents and abilities by encouraging and allowing them access to a variety of activities.

Naturally, we gravitate to social activities, athletics, political groups, technical areas, and the arts if we have experienced some degree of success or stimulation in these areas or if we want to emulate someone else. Involvement in new activities is often intimidating, but we have to get out of our comfort zone and explore new ventures. Many times opportunities are thrust upon us by chance, and we find our niche; at other times parents have their own ideas about what they think is good for us, and they may encourage our participation. Teachers may also notice areas in which we excel. Young people need to be encouraged to try a variety of activities in order to find something of interest to them.

Options

An abundance of extracurricular opportunities are available for school-aged students. By junior high/middle school, many young people have had ample opportunities to experience activities offered in the community, at school, or through family exposure. Adults need to encourage and support young people's involvement in many different types of activities. Young people should look within themselves and be encouraged to try healthy activities that they like or want to learn more about.

Community and school resources need to be utilized if there are financial concerns. Many clubs, groups, and organizations require an activity, equipment, or registration fee, as well as medical exams and adequate insurance. Students can also solicit assistance from appropriate adult role models, school sponsors, or community leaders. Many of us limit participation to activities that interest our peers or our parents and siblings. Black students need to avoid stereotypical activities and seek participation in the most challenging events and activities. Sometimes I excelled at or tried activities that had appealed to none of my friends. As a result, I had some great experiences that none of my friends had ever thought about. Even today as an adult, many of my friends have never had the opportunities I have been fortunate to experience. I never want to say, "I wish I had . . ." or "I should have done it when I had the chance."

Leadership Development

Most people join activities to feel the thrill and excitement of participation and to satisfy their need to belong and be accepted. If we select activities that involve others, we must experience a certain protocol or rite of passage. This includes getting to know others and working cooperatively with a team of people with similar interests. Individual-activity participation involves a different type of mental discipline because we may act solo, though we are still part of a team. Leadership development involves a serious mind-set with intense time commitments.

If you have the natural ability to lead, then you are more inclined to seek leadership roles. Not everyone needs to aspire to leadership, but individuals can be active participants and benefit from leadership qualities. Such persons may be more of a behind-the-scenes type or function in a supportive role. In actuality, this role is critical to the overall success of any project. It is important that students develop leadership qualities that will assist them in being successful and responsible individuals.

Values

My parents had a healthy perspective about my involvement in athletics, student leadership positions, and social organizations. They along with my other "role models," coaches, teachers, and family members, helped me develop the attitude that success means more than just defeating others and that losing did not mean failing. I may not have realized it when I was in junior high/middle school, but they taught me that the most important kind of success resides in personal improvement, giving maximum effort, and commitment to doing one's best at all times.

Young people may not know the value of achieving goals unless they learn how to define their own standards and abilities. I was most heavily involved in athletics as a primary extracurricular activity, especially track and field. I enjoyed the competition, and I liked the interaction with others. I began competing in track and field when I was in elementary school, excelling throughout high school, and this ability allowed me to continue competing on the college level. Undoubtedly, there is enormous pressure to perform at a certain level, for most extracurricular activities are very competitive among both team members and with other schools. This is a time of continued development athletically, academically, socially, physically, and emotionally, and this is also a time when peer relationships are extremely important.

Young students need to be able to interpret and understand their role as extracurricular activity participants in a healthy and self-enhancing way. Often, young people become angry and frustrated with themselves or others when they make a mistake, and they risk losing their concentration and composure. Parents, teachers, and coaches have to create a supportive atmosphere that allows young people to view their mistakes as a natural part of learning. We all need to learn or relearn how to accept our own personal limitations gracefully without destroying the motivation to continue participating.

Black high school students especially need people involved in their lives to be supportive, knowledgeable, encouraging, instructive, honest, sincere, fair, consistent, enthusiastic, and fun to provide constructive guidance. Extracurricular activities are a wonderful vehicle for developing confidence and self-esteem. However, this is not the only avenue that defines an individual's personal identity; it is just one part of an individual's many unique qualities and characteristics.

Benefits

Consistent participation in extracurricular activities provides numerous overall benefits. As an adult, I am able to analyze past interactions, specific occasions, and unique relations that have assisted in molding the person I have become. Many different influences shape our character. The skills I acquired during my formative years have helped me to achieve success as an adult. Even today I am willing to try new and different things, some of which are considered culture or gender specific.

I am willing to go beyond stereotypical barriers and to explore and take chances because I may never have the opportunity to do it again. I became involved in many different activities, some of which lasted longer than others, but I emerged and excelled as a sportsperson. My athletic achievements, the many friends I have made, my opportunities to travel, and the unique experiences I've had are priceless. I earned respect from members of my community and at the schools I attended not necessarily because I excelled in track, but because as I matured I was a likable, caring, and reliable person. I was also an excellent student. The question I pose to young people I interact with is this: "How do you know what your interests are or what you are good at if you never try or never expose yourself to anything?"

CONCLUSION

Extracurricular activities are just that—extra things we do along with our required daily activities. We have interest in these activities, and perhaps we are good at them; however, for most activities you only have to be dedicated and hard working. We are not all great at everything we set out to do, but getting involved allows us to experience many things that will assist us in being successful. Success can mean many things to many people. For black students extracurricular activities are what is necessary to provide the avenue for us to showcase our many talents and abilities that can go unnoticed. Students need to be assertive now so that they can develop their critical thinking skills.

Extracurricular activities bring out the best in young people, offering them an opportunity for learning and for supplementing classroom instruction. Experiencing success builds satisfaction and self-confidence. The result, increased self-esteem, can and often results in enhanced academic performance as well. Extracurricular participation encourages self-discipline. Black students can learn the value of identifying appropriate behaviors and adhering to them throughout every changing and challenging aspect of their lives.

The discipline it takes to be committed in extra activities encourages regular routines to achieve excellence and success. A philosophy of extracurricular activities as an extension of the classroom is necessary to give the black high school student clear direction for academic, social, and emotional success.

Charles Van Gunn, Jr.
Louisiana State University High School, Baton Rouge,
Louisiana

As a sixteen-year-old honor student at Louisiana State University High School in Baton Rouge, Louisiana, I have found the high school experience to be a challenging and most enjoyable one. I have made many new friends and engaged in a number of fun activities. In May of 1997, I should graduate from University High with honors.

I attribute my success in high school to several factors, one major one being a supportive family. My mother finished law school while I was in junior high school, and so she understood the need to study and made sure I devoted my time to it. Throughout the history of my family, it has been taught that education is a necessary tool for success in life. Therefore, education has never been viewed as optional but mandatory. The unspoken rule is that after high school, you enroll in college.

My participation in extracurricular activities has also contributed to my success in high school. I have played soccer since preschool, and I have been in the band since elementary school. My participation in these and other extracurricular activities has not only sharpened my skills, but also promoted a more positive feeling about myself. I feel good about myself when I play my trumpet in a concert or when I either win or lose a game. The mere fact that I am part of these activities boosts my self-esteem. Participation has also increased my number of friends and deepened many of my friendships. Being on a team and working toward a common goal have made my relationships stronger.

Being friendly to my peers seems to make them friendlier toward me. When I take an interest in the kids at school, they seem to repay me with the same interest. I make sure that I do not have a chip on my shoulder when I go to school, because I want to project a positive image at all times. Because of my personality, I have become very popular on campus, and I take pride in the fact that I treat other people the way I want to be treated.

Also contributing to my success in high school has been my willingness to stop procrastinating and to get my work done. I put my school work first in the afternoons. After carefully writing my assignments while in class, I diligently work to complete them when I get home. Delaying my work only creates a problem for me, because I usually forget the unwritten details of the assignment or I fail to go the extra mile in completing it. Procrastination works against me.

Finally, keeping my career goal before me has helped to keep me on track. I plan to be a computer engineer, and I know what it takes to achieve this goal. I am reminded of my career goal each time I take an exam and each time I write a paper. I tell myself that I must make good grades in order to be accepted into my chosen degree program in college, and I find myself making connections with persons who are knowledgeable about my chosen area.

All of these factors have enhanced my success in high school. I feel positive about myself and about my future, and I am happy and content.

CHAPTER 8

Leadership In and Out of the Classroom

RUBY D. HIGGINS

Assistant Director of Multicultural Affairs, Student Opportunities and Services, University of Nebraska, Lincoln

Leadership is the process by which one individual influences others to accomplish desired goals. Leadership skills are among the most useful and rewarding skills an individual can possess. They will be important not only at the present time in your life, but in the future as well. High school is a perfect time to experiment with and develop your leadership skills. Each person possesses certain innate leadership skills but needs to establish and improve upon various others. The leadership skills that you develop in high school will prove to be extremely valuable in the years to come. When you successfully complete high school and choose to attend an institution of higher learning or enter the workforce, the more leadership skills you possess the better the opportunities you will have. Graduate schools and employers look for leadership skills. Academic institutions and employers want individuals who will take charge and develop themselves to their full potential. These individuals help the institution or employer to achieve success.

Secondary schools and higher education institutions promote leadership and prepare leaders for our society. A few institutions have leadership in their mission, motto, and curriculum. High school is a training ground for leadership. Many students go to college after having participated in leadership activities in high school. Several higher education institutions emphasize leadership development alongside career preparation. Schools like Morehouse College train students for leadership in society. The only private African-American institution for men, Morehouse produces graduates who are expected to take leadership roles in their community, state, region, and country. Many men in education, business, and government are products of "The House." It is important to remember that high schools prepare students for the leadership opportunities that make it possible to attend institutions like Morehouse.

Basically, there are two kinds of leaders: those who take on formal leadership roles and those who act as leaders in an informal manner. A formal leader is someone who is officially invested with organizational authority and power, and is a take-charge type of person. This leader is generally referred to as "the boss" and dictates tasks and responsibilities to other workers. Such leaders have a great deal of responsibility and must be careful to portray the right image to others and to cultivate productive relationships. Often a leader's success is dependent on how well he or she delegates authority and responsibility. How well the individuals working for this person carry out their instructions often determines the leader's ultimate success.

An informal leader does not have an official leadership title but exercises a leadership function all the same, influencing others through personal attributes or superior performance. For example, a principal at a high school may distribute job duties to his or her faculty and staff. Each teacher may receive the same instructions, but one or several may decide to take on a larger leadership role. A certain teacher may decide to develop a committee on science curriculum, thus taking on a leadership role in assisting other teachers in the curriculum selection process. These leaders are crucial in establishing effective organizations. Informal leaders often do not want all the attention and responsibilities that formal leaders have and therefore choose to lead by gathering others and acting as assistants to others who have official responsibility. Informal leadership roles are excellent for developing leadership skills and frequently lead to formal leadership opportunities.

Are leaders born or developed? The "Great Man Theory," one of the first leadership theories promoted, states that great men are born, not trained. Modern theories of leadership acknowledge that leadership skills can in fact be developed. Remember that African Americans have a strong legacy of leadership. Our ancestry is rich in documentation of leaders in all walks of life.

High school is an excellent place to learn and acquire leadership skills. Many students become involved in leadership activities in classrooms and school organizations, as well as in the neighborhood or community. Leaders come in all shapes and sizes, from diverse economic situations, and exhibit differences in vision, skills, and abilities. Leadership does not have any specific forum within which it can operate. You can be the president of the student body, captain or co-captain of an athletic team, or the chair of a committee working on a class project.

The Characteristics of Leadership

The following is a list of some traits that are commonly identified as being highly correlated with leadership (Bothwell, 1988).

1. Intelligence.
2. Ability to motivate self and others.
3. Ability to get along with others.

4. Planning and organizational skills.

5. Strong desire to achieve tasks by using abilities to be effective and efficient.

6. Emotional stability and self-control.

7. Ability to use the group process.

8. Decisiveness.

Whatever individual traits leaders may have, there are two qualities that set true leaders apart: they have a dream they are determined to see carried out, and they are not just dreamers but people of action. Results are produced by action that often inspires others to act. Single acts that produce collective acts change the world. To be a true leader, you must have a vision and act to bring it about.

Leadership involves the use of power. Leaders must understand what power is, where it comes from, and how it is used or abused (Bothwell, 1988). To lead is to exercise power. Power means the ability to

Make things happen

Influence people

Influence events

Create change

Produce results

Don't let anyone try to fool you. Without power, people cannot make things happen. If nothing happens, we have no leadership, no personal success, no progress. Both in and out of the classroom, leadership is very important. Whether it is in school or the community, the state, or the nation, being a leader has tangible and intangible benefits.

You can be a leader in your classroom. Many young people are apprehensive about being school leaders because they feel their peers may reject them for their interests. However, many others look up to leaders and will view you as a prized person. Leaders are sought after by organizations and institutions. People value your efforts and successes. Being a leader, though not always easy, is worthwhile. It is worth it when you receive awards and scholarships; it is worth it when you don't have to worry about paying fees to college; it is worth it when you are introduced to successful and highly regarded individuals who applaud you for your hard work, perseverance, and success. Because you produce results, being a classroom leader is worth the difficulties you may face.

High school presents many leadership opportunities, and it is important that you start in an environment that is comfortable for you. First, you must find an organization that interests you. Guidance counselors, faculty, staff, and other students can provide you with many different options. Upon finding groups you are interested in, you should attend meetings, get involved, participate in special events, and determine whether you support the group's objectives. When you have joined the group(s) you are interested in, you should recognize how you can become a leader within that group. Do what you can to help strengthen its structure and bring excitement, new ideas, hard work, and leadership to achieve results.

Being a student government leader gives you an opportunity to talk to students, teachers, school and district administrators, parents, and civic leaders about issues affecting students in your high school. You can create change in the current system. As a byproduct, you will develop and refine your communication skills, and develop skills in group dynamics and conflict resolution.

As a leader in other school groups, you can influence and educate others through your delivery of information. If you are the Math or Science Club president, you may be able to present a difficult subject to the student population in a way that is clear, entertaining, and educational. You gain the respect and acceptance of your peers, as you influence them.

It is important that you not limit yourself to leadership opportunities related exclusively to school groups. Many other opportunities exist at the community, state, and national levels. Community groups such as the United Way, NAACP, UNCF, and others are all excellent. Church groups and countless numbers of volunteer agencies are always looking for good leaders to help accomplish their goals. If you have an interest that none of the groups seems to be addressing, don't be afraid to start your own. By becoming involved with various organizations, you position yourself to become exposed to a number of different organizational structures. Each structure possesses unique leadership positions, opportunities, and contrasting leadership styles. Involvement with numerous groups allows you to learn a great deal about these structures and begin to develop your own set of leadership skills.

The community organization leader is able to represent the view of the younger citizens. The organization may be social, civic, or religious, and you can make a difference. The one element that is constant in life is change. People don't always want to do the same things the same way. Your ideas, suggestions, and recommendations may influence decisions that impact the community. You create change and make things happen.

For a moment, let us look at negative leadership. Unfortunately, more and more young people are joining gangs. Gangs are viewed negatively because they violate the law, treat people horrifically, and destroy property. The structure of the gang is similar to that of any other organization, and its leaders operate by power. The difference is that their influence is negative; they do not provide positive role models for young people. Leaders shape the culture of an organization. Positive leaders are role models through their own behavior. They have certain goals and objectives, and they accomplish them by working openly with others who may or may not fully agree with their ideas. This positive leadership often involves compromise and fosters positive relationships with other groups.

Successful leadership is not automatic. Sometimes those in

leadership roles fail miserably, but failure should not be used as an excuse to give up becoming a leader. Rework your position and procedure. Learn from past experiences—both successes and failures—and determine why you succeeded or failed. Try also to learn from the past experiences of others. If you see others make mistakes, analyze the situation and identify alternatives. Test these alternatives when the opportunities are available. When opportunities to serve in leadership roles present themselves, you should accept the challenge. Developing leaders are

Inquisitive
Energetic
Responsible
Courageous
Spontaneous

In addition, consider opportunities for leadership training and development. Your high school may offer a course in leadership, which will allow you to learn about different leadership styles and have the chance to interact with students of various backgrounds, interests, and leadership abilities. Weekend or evening seminars at local community colleges, learning centers, or community agencies are also good places to gain leadership training and experience. Another option is to visit your local library or bookstore. Countless numbers of books and videotapes are available for you to explore at your own pace. These tools often provide excellent advice and suggestions for developing leadership skills and give tips on how to get involved as well.

Finally, know your personal strengths and weakness, and try to know those of others. Know the limits of your skills, abilities, and interests, but do not be intimidated by them. Seek to expand yourself by constant challenge. Young African Americans in high schools are leaders in the rough. As the current leadership matures, you must be ready to take their place. You must conscientiously and deliberately prepare, both in and out of the classroom, for the challenges of society.

REFERENCE

Bothwell, L. (1988). *The Art of Leadership*. New York: Prentice-Hall.

Bianca Bellock
Xavier Prep High School, Marrero, Louisiana

Taking the initiative to stand on one's own beliefs and morals, and demonstrating one's convictions through everyday actions are both very difficult goals for any young person today. Choosing to uphold the morally just against the opposition of negativity and peer pressure is becoming ever more difficult for students. Because of the particular pressures young African Americans are now facing, it is imperative that they prepare themselves mentally and academically for the challenges that lie ahead. One of the most important aspects of this preparation is the development of leadership skills.

A true leader is not simply one who leads others. Rather, a leader is one who sets precedents, laying a solid foundation and providing a sense of direction for those who are searching to make their way in life. All the qualities of a good leader come from within; these qualities include a sound sense of oneself, integrity, a willingness to teach as well as a willingness to learn from others, tenacity, and a thirst for knowledge. With these qualities, being a leader becomes synonymous with achieving success in high school. Believing in one's own judgment is a vital tool when one is faced with limitless options that stray from the straight and narrow. Remaining focused is also essential for scholastic achievement. Having the ability to plan ahead and to organize are also leadership skills necessary for success in high school. Interactions with people are part of everyday life, both in and out of school, and are important in producing a successful leader. Effective time management and consistent followup are imperative for planning and completing assignments on time. Being a leader is a responsibility that should be taken seriously, just as school should be taken seriously. Leadership is an integral part of academics, and anyone who plans to embark on the journey that leads to high school success should enthusiastically embrace strong leadership skills. These skills should be incorporated and become part of a student's everyday life. If one is able to exercise these qualities where school is concerned and work continuously to improve every day, success will be within easy reach.

CHAPTER 9

Making the Smart Choice: Say No to Drugs, Alcohol, Crime, and Pregnancy

WILTON A. BARHAM

Associate Professor, Educational Leadership and Habilitative Services, Grambling State University, Grambling, Louisiana

As a black high school student, you are expected to make some of the same difficult choices your parents had to make when they were your age. However, unlike your parents in their youth, you are living in an open and advanced society in which you are exposed to a mountain of information from many different sources, especially television, the print media, and the movies. Thus, life is more difficult and challenging for you. Nor have you had the sheltered upbringing that most of your parents had when they were high school students. Thus, you are expected to make smart choices from many more alternatives if you are to be successful in your experiences.

I would like to share some information with you about four choices that will confront you on a daily basis: (1) Selling, using, and abusing uncontrolled or illegal drugs; (2) using and abusing alcoholic beverages; (3) engaging in criminal activities;

and (4) participating in premarital sexual activities that lead to pregnancy. Not coincidentally, these are also the four great social issues of our time.

Choices related to these four areas are documented to be among the most important factors that will impact your success as young black high school students. The abuse of drugs and alcohol, the effect of crime, and the negative consequences of pregnancy are considered to be the greatest challenges to the civility and progress of our modern society. But why am I talking to you about this subject, you might ask? I bring it up precisely because the consequences of your choices can be very life-threatening and can contribute to high school failure. Your choices can undermine or strengthen the moral fiber of our society; they can weaken or reinforce the instruction, exhortation, and training in good habits that you have received in the home, school, and community.

Choices imply the possibility of having alternatives or the opportunity or privilege of choosing freely. As we discuss the alternatives of drugs, alcohol, crime, and pregnancy, we are reminded that a rationale must exist for our choices and that once these choices are made, consequences are inevitable. Indeed, for all choices we make in life (far more than the four we are discussing here), there are positive and negative consequences. In other words, we must consciously think of the reason(s) for every choice we make in life. Are you aware of the consequences, and have they contributed positively to your success in high school? In making choices, everyone must be guided by several virtues of life: self-discipline, responsibility, work, and courage. These values play a central role in your decision to make or not make drugs, alcohol, crime, or pregnancy part of your high school experiences. How well you embrace these values will determine how smart your choices will be.

Drugs and Your High School Success

Almost everyone will agree that drug abuse threatens our nation's youth. Let me share some startling statistics with you: The average age of initial marijuana use has dropped to 11 (Towers, 1987); during a thirty-day period in 1985, 30 percent of high school seniors used marijuana and 15 percent snorted cocaine (Tarlov & Rimel, 1986); teenage drug use in the United States in 1986 was the highest in any industrialized nation (U.S. Department of Education, 1986). More recently, in 1991, a study conducted in Milwaukee, Wisconsin, reported that only 26 percent of 194 African-American, Southeast-Asian, Hispanic, Native American, and white adolescents had never used drugs (Social Development Commission, 1992). The annual teen drug study at the University of Michigan reported that after thirteen years of decline, marijuana (pot) use is on the rise again: 16.5 percent of tenth graders in 1991 to 34.7 percent in 1995 (Guttman, 1996). The same study also indicated the trend in marijuana use for high school seniors: 50.8 percent in 1979, 38.8 percent in 1986, 21.9 percent in 1992, and 34.7 percent in 1995.

Why are you or some of your friends selling and using marijuana, heroin, cocaine, and crack? Using drugs in the company of friends was a primary recreational activity for 40 percent of those interviewed in the Milwaukee study. For some, weak familial and school attachments may increase the likelihood of exposure to drug social influences. Other reasons may be lower resistance; self-efficacy; peer pressure; lack of a positive school atmosphere; or poor self-esteem (Ellickson & Hays, 1992). Here are the reasons two former high school users of marijuana (a Hispanic and a black) gave for using marijuana: "I wanted to be accepted and it was cool," and "I only smoked for a few months. . . . I thought marijuana was no big deal" (Guttman, 1996). A number of cultural factors are influencing young Americans to use pot. For example, today marijuana is openly promoted at concerts, on television, on music videos and CDs, and even on T-shirts. This message of social acceptance is the wrong message that society is sending to you and your friends. You must not embrace it!

Despite the problems that you encounter because of any of the situations described earlier, the selling or use of drugs is not an appropriate response or solution. Such behavior has serious consequences for you and other members of our society. Indeed, the use of marijuana is a big deal. The following consequences have been demonstrated by the experts, and you ought to be aware of them.

Drug abuse is linked to dropping out of school, depression, suicide, and violence. By dropping out of school, you will not receive the educational preparation that will allow you to live a worthwhile life and thus make a positive contribution to the quality of life in this country and the world. The use of drugs can have a negative effect on your learning: Researcher Susan Hooper (1988) has informed us that "scientific research has shown that many drugs, even when taken in small doses, can cause permanent damage to the learning centers of the brain— damage which increases with increased drug use." In addition, marijuana reduces coordination, slows reflexes, interferes with the ability to measure distance, speed, and time, and disrupts concentration and short-term memory. A marijuana smoker is exposed to six times as many carcinogens as a tobacco smoker (Guttman, 1996). So you can see that drug use is not a smart choice!

How can you end any current involvement or avoid any experiences with drugs? You must rely on yourself, your family, and your community. With regards to yourself, you must develop or continue to develop sound values of self-discipline, responsibility, work, and courage. According to former Education Secretary William Bennett, in self-discipline one makes a "disciple" of oneself (Bennett, 1993). He goes on to say that one is one's own teacher, trainer, coach and "disciplinarian." Successful everyday behavior, such as avoidance of drug use, requires that we exert a great amount of self-discipline. In other words, each of us must control our passions, appetite, or impulses which could threaten our well-being and the well-being of others. For us to be responsible, we must be accountable. Dr. Bennett reminds us that responsible persons are mature individuals who have taken charge of themselves and their conduct. If you are responsible for your actions, you cannot blame your peers for influencing your choice to use drugs. Instead, you should avoid drug abuse by focusing on the goal of achieving an excellent high school education. A sense of responsibility can be developed if you complete household chores, do your homework as assigned, participate in extra-curricular activities, secure after-school jobs, and volunteer to work in community organizations. The work or effort that is involved in these activities is more meaningful than being engaged in the selling or use of illicit drugs. And then, there is courage: standing our ground against that which threatens our health and success. It requires much courage to resist the temptations that lead to destructive behavior. I do agree with William Bennett that you will need wisdom to give your courage determinate form and intelligent direction.

This wisdom can come from your teachers, parents, and community leaders. By providing improved information, referral, outreach services, and a curriculum that explores culturally based values, teachers will help you to become wiser. However, you cannot benefit from their support if you do not participate in the programs that are available; you must seek out and participate in the learning activities of your school. Your parents are usually better sources of information about the dangers of drug abuse than your peers. Even if your parent or parents experimented with marijuana in the 1960s, you must listen to them in the 1990s: they are saying that they were foolish and that they do not want you to use marijuana or any other form of illicit drugs. In the event you cannot rely on them because of their acceptance of the abuse of drugs or their ignorance of the consequences, then you must rely on your teachers or community leaders. All three groups—teachers, parents, and community leaders—must form a team to educate you, and you should develop the confidence necessary to benefit from their guidance. I did benefit from the wisdom of my teachers, parents, and community leaders, especially our social and religious leaders. You can benefit too!

Ultimately, you have to rely on your strength of character and your purpose in life. That is, (1) you must continuously resist the temptation to see marijuana as harmless, even a healthful alternative to cigarettes and alcohol; (2) you must reject some parents' acceptance of the use of dope (marijuana); (3) you must recognize that pot is not endorsed by a majority of adults even if Vice President Al Gore or House Speaker Newt Gingrich have tried it; (4) you must resist being influenced by the images you see on television; and (5) you should develop an interest outside the classroom such as sports, music, or participation in a voluntary organization and vigorously pursue that interest. Always think of the negative consequences of drug use, such as the disruption in your high school education, the bad effects on your health, or incarceration in juvenile detention centers or jails. Schools will no longer protect drug abusers; in addition to the provision of support, they have instituted tough rules against the selling and use of drugs that could lead to expulsion and convictions. These rules have the strong support of parents and the larger community.

Alcohol and High School Success

Many of your peers are engaging in a very unhealthy lifestyle. Why is this so? Again, you hear students saying that they are doing it to be noticed, to be liked by their peers, or to be cool. Also, because it is a legal drug for certain age groups, many minors for whom it is an illegal drug find themselves abusing it; they believe they are mature enough to use it safely. Others take it for simple pleasure; because of peer pressure; in order to experiment; as a response to the constant exposure to our chemical society of pills and liquor through advertisements,

movies, and television; or to rebel against the greed, materi-
alism, and get-ahead-at-any-cost attitude that some of your
colleagues think your parents' generation personifies (Guttman, 1996).

As is true of drugs, costly results are associated with the
abuse of alcohol. For example, automobile accidents caused by
drivers who are under the influence of alcohol are the leading
cause of death and injuries among adolescents in the United
States. Furthermore, the combination of drug and alcohol
abuse can lead to physical problems, emotional damage, and
a decline in educational achievement and productivity (Barrett,
1986). Often drug and alcohol abusers tend to skip or arrive
late to class. Experimentation with drugs and alcohol, particularly at a young age, will often lead to dependence. To satisfy
this dependence, some of your peers steal, sell drugs to others,
and engage in prostitution.

Is using alcohol a smart choice? Without question, the overwhelming evidence suggests that this is *not* a smart choice for
you or your friends. Again, you must help get out the message
that alcohol use and abuse is dangerous to your health. You
are encouraged to participate in such programs as the San An-
tonio-based "Fighting Back" program in which teens tell one
another that they show disrespect to their community when
they take the risk of using something that lowers their inhibi-
tions (Guttman, 1996). This is an example of taking personal
responsibility for your actions and at the same time contributing to the safety and good health of your community.

Crime and High School Success

As I indicated earlier, participation in criminal activities by
high school students is generally linked to the need to satisfy
their drug habit. It usually starts with stealing, the so-called
petty crime, and later, if a gun is used in the commission of a
crime, it can escalate to homicide. Firearms possession and

drugs among inner-city high school students were the subject of a study by J. F. Sheley in 1994. Data were collected from male inner-city high school students pertaining to firearms possession; use of heroin, cocaine, and crack; drug selling; and commission of crimes with weapons. Data analysis reveals a progressive, linear relationship between level of drug use and gun possession. In a Youth Risk Behavior Survey of 1,412 high school students in Colorado in 1991, nearly one-half of the male students indicated that they had carried a weapon within the past thirty days, and one-third of all respondents reported having tried marijuana; 19 percent said they had tried other illicit drugs (Colorado State Department of Education, 1992). While no commission of crimes was reported in these two studies, the possession of weapons and the use of drugs create the climate for crimes to occur. These behaviors are not healthy for our young people, and it is clear that students in Colorado and other states in our nation must change their behavior if high school is to be successful for them.

How can young people change their risky behavior? In addition to what I have already suggested, they must embrace "Saying No" to drugs and anticrime programs that will teach them to resist peer pressure by understanding and practicing reasons for not taking drugs and engaging in criminal activities (Lachance, 1985). You should join these "Just Say No" clubs where you will have a reason and a way to say no to these poor choices. As a high school student, I benefited from participation in sports and various social clubs; I learned positive lifestyles by working with adults and peers who modeled these lifestyles. My friends and I were constantly reminded that we would be unable to meet our academic goals if we engaged in risky behaviors. In addition, we were fortunate to have the guidance of our village: we were trained by parents, teachers, and the responsible members of our community because they wanted us to succeed and they shared in our success. You too have the chance to be successful if you embrace the message of hope and seize the opportunities that a high school education will provide for you.

Pregnancy and High School Success

Finally, I want to discuss with you the heartbreak and pain, the lost hope and opportunity, and the economic hardship experienced by the pregnant high school girl. The same Colorado high school survey revealed that over one-half of the students surveyed were sexually active; 10 percent of high school seniors had been pregnant or caused a pregnancy; and 23 to 39 percent of sexually active students used alcohol.

Why are some of your peers engaging in sexual intercourse at such a young age? Some have said that they are doing so because of unfulfilled needs; some girls report that older boys and men take advantage of them; and both genders say that they wanted to learn about sex earlier than is expected. Some are victims of poor economic circumstances that can contribute to sexual activity. In earlier decades, these were some of the same reasons given by many young pregnant women in this and similar societies. Indeed, every generation has had to deal with this problem. In addition, in 1995 the news magazine *CNN Reports* revealed that a national crisis is looming; young people are having sex earlier and are becoming pregnant earlier than at any other time in our nation's history.

Pregnant students are often left to care for their babies alone or with little help from their parents; the fathers do not usually offer any support. The young mothers generally have to drop out of school, thus interrupting or ending their high school education. The economic hardship of taking care of a baby without gainful employment, and the consequences mentioned earlier result in personal tragedy for many young women.

As in the case of drug and alcohol and crime, many pregnancies result in a tremendous social and economic cost to society in the form of aid to dependent children and other economic support programs, and an undereducated or uneducated population. To be successful high school students, you must join in the many community efforts to adopt new ways of thinking and behavior in order to prevent premarital sex, which may lead to unwanted pregnancies.

Becoming sexually active is the wrong way to respond to unfulfilled needs. If you feel the need to be loved, wanted, or secure, you should discuss these needs with your parents, teachers, or church leaders. Parenthood requires a great deal of maturity, and at this young age and with little experience, it is a great responsibility to care for a baby. You can benefit by becoming involved with youth groups sponsored by your school or church in which many of your questions relating to human sexuality, situational ethics, and morality can be answered. At this age, young boys and girls should continue to focus on developing their academic skills, young girls should develop friendships with other girls, and everyone should develop relationships with their parents.

CONCLUSION

By now, it should be clear that selling, using, and abusing drugs or alcohol, committing criminal acts, and engaging in premarital sexual activity that will lead to pregnancies are not smart choices. They are poor alternatives for fulfilling needs and desires, or for achieving success in high school and beyond; choosing any of them will lead to destructive behavior.

If you take responsibility for your actions and are influenced by your parents, teachers, community leaders, or other positive role models, you will always be successful. Responsibility must also be accompanied by self-discipline, hard work, and courage. These values, along with strength of character and constant focus on your goals, will serve you well in this complex world.

You must also rely on support outside of yourself, such as the development of strong family ties and a closer relationship with your school, church, and other agencies in your community that promote positive and healthy lifestyles. In addition, you should participate in sports, band, or voluntary organizations, secure an after-school job, or engage in tutorial or academic enhancement activities. These activities, and others, are excellent alternatives to drugs, alcohol, crime and pregnancy. They are *smart choices*.

REFERENCES

Barrett, J. (1986). *Drug Abuse: Prevention Strategies for Schools*. Washington, DC: ERIC Clearinghouse on Teacher Education. (ERIC Document Reproduction Services No. ED 279 644).

Bennett, W. J., ed. (1993). *The Book of Virtues: A Treasury of Great Moral Stories*. New York: Simon and Schuster.

Colorado State Department of Education. (1992). *Colorado: Youth Risk Behavior Survey, 1991*. Denver, Colo.: Colorado State Department of Education and Colorado University Health Sciences Center. (ERIC Document Reproduction Services No. ED 359 469).

D'Andrea, M. (1990). *Applied Research and Counseling Practice: A Comprehensive Strategy to Promote the Prevention of Adolescent Pregnancies Among Underclass Youth*. (ERIC Document Reproduction Services No. ED 324 582).

Ellickson, P. J., and R. D. Hays (1992). "On Becoming Involved with Drugs: Modeling Adolescent Drug Use Over Time." *Journal of Health Psychology* 11 (6): 377–385.

Guttman, M. (1996, February 16–18). "The New Pot Culture." *USA Weekend*, pp. 4–7.

Hooper, S. (1988). *Alcohol and Drugs in the Public Schools: Implications for School Leaders*. Alexandria, Va.: National School Boards Association.

Klauke, A. (1988). *Stopping Drug Use*. Eugene, Oreg.: ERIC Clearinghouse on Educational Management. (ERIC Document Reproduction Services No. ED 301 968).

Lachance, L. L. (1985). *Substance Abuse Prevention in Schools*. (ERIC Document Reproduction Services No. ED 264 502).

Sheley, J. F. (1994). "Drugs and Guns Among Inner-City High School Students." *Journal of Drug Education* 24 (4): 303–321.

Social Development Commission. (1992). *Fighting Back: The Cultural Context of Drug and Alcohol Use Among Youth*. Milwaukee, Wis.: Author. (ERIC Document Reproduction Service No. ED 353 517).

Tarlov, A. R., and R. W. Rimel. (1986). "Drug Abuse Prevention—The Sponsoring Foundations Perspective." *Journal of School Health* 56: 358.

Towers, R. L. (1987). *How Schools Can Help Combat Student Drug and Alcohol Abuse*. Washington, DC: National Education Association of the United States.

U.S. Department of Education (1986). *Schools Without Drugs*. Washington, DC: (ERIC Document Reproduction Services No. ED 270 715).

Rehema N. Githiga
Grambling State University, Grambling, Louisiana

Consuming alcohol is a very popular activity among teens, and it is not easy to find many of my peers who do not drink some kind of alcohol. Drinking is brought about mainly by peer pressure. That means that drinking students try to find a student whom they know will fall into their trap of pressure.

Being a teen in the 1990s is not easy because adults have labeled us as destructive. Also, we are known as Generation X, a generation with no future. Personally, I dealt with the pressure by talking with my parents and sitting alone and trying to find out where I stand as an individual. When my peers would go out to drink, I would always drink something other than what they were drinking. At first, they saw my actions as trying to be a "pretty girl," but if you explain yourself and show them that you have a mind of your own, they will respect your values and what you stand for.

Parents always say, "find a good, clean friend" in today's world, but it's hard to find that perfect friend. You have to work on your friendship and tell each other what you expect in the friendship. As I grew older and wiser, things began to fall into place. Most of my peers whom I considered my "friends" showed their true colors later down the road when I tried to explain that their drinking was going overboard, and that they should consider stopping because they were falling behind in their class work. They turned to me and said that it was none of my concern and that I should just "let them be." After that confrontation, I went home and asked my mother whether I had done the right thing. She told me that if they were my true friends, they would have seen it as a concern, and not as being judgmental. When I went back to school and talked to the boys and asked them whether they would like a girl who drinks, the response was not a surprise: they all said no, they wouldn't want a girl who drinks. Then I asked, "Why do you go on drinking with the girls or even ask them if they want to drink?" They said they just want to see which girl has a mind of her own, one who doesn't follow the crowd.

With the help of my parents and the love of God instilled in me, I consider myself a strong black lady who can stand for what she thinks is right and not look back. My personal message to every young girl and boy is as the famous Charles Kingsley said: "There are two freedoms: the false where a man is free to do what he likes; the true where a man is free to do what he ought."

CHAPTER 10

Choosing Your Friends

STEPHEN PEMBERTON
Associate Director of Undergraduate Admissions, Boston College

It is highly fashionable these days to talk about role models for African-American students. Everywhere you turn, you hear discussions about who your role models should be or even if there are any role models worthy of your admiration. Lost in all of this conversation is that group of people who (after your parents and family) will have a significant impact on your life—your friends. I do not mean to diminish the importance of role models, for they are critical to the African-American student. However, on a day-to-day basis our friends affect and influence us in a way that is far different from role models and family. It is my hope that after reading this chapter you will have a clearer understanding of what friendship means and some important things to consider when choosing your friends.

If you were to look up the definition of *friend*, you would find that *Webster's Dictionary* defines *friend* as "one attached to another by affection and esteem." Although that definition rings true when we think of our friends, it does not help us that much when we consider how we choose our friends.

Choosing your friends is just that—a choice—and the first and most important consideration in choosing your friends is *yourself*. To the best of my knowledge, no book has ever been written that states that your friends have to be a certain group of people. However, your friends are an extension of you; therefore, choosing your friends does indeed begin with you.

Even though you may feel it is too early, high school is a time and a place where you will make decisions that will affect the rest of your life. What are your plans for the future? What would you like to become? What college would you like to attend? Even if you do not have the answers to these questions, they are still important to ask because they give you a sense of direction, and having a vision for your future is essential in choosing your friends. Your decision as to who your friends will be throughout your high school career should reflect your long-term goals. That is not to say that all of your friends should be identical, but they certainly should not distract or deter from your vision of your future.

Your friends are also a reflection of yourself. There is an old saying that bears repeating here: "You can tell a great deal about a person by looking at that person's friends." To a large extent, we are often associated with those people we call our friends, and those associations can be positive or negative. One of the best pieces of advice I received was from my mentor, Mrs. Dottin, who cautioned me: "*Do not allow people to choose you as their friend, but be sure that you choose your friends.*" As I look back on my own high school years, I believe that one of the wisest choices I made was to listen to that advice. On most occasions those individuals who sought to choose me as their friend were headed in a direction that was profoundly different from my own. When I chose my friends (keeping in mind my own goals), my friendships were far more beneficial.

I believe that the term *friend* is an often overused and misunderstood expression. Often we use the term *friend* casually without fully understanding its complete meaning, and that is the reason why I would caution you to distinguish between a friend and an acquaintance. Friendships are a process and not a statement one makes. There are certain characteristics that mark a friendship that you would not often see in an acquaintance. Friendships are relationships in which you have

1. ***Trust*** and ***confidence*** in one another.

   These feelings develop with time and come with the knowledge that the person you choose as your friend is someone you can depend on as well as confide in. You should never question your ability to trust or confide in someone you call a friend.

2. The ability to ***be yourself*** without concerns about peer pressure.

   Being yourself can be difficult, and yet among friends being yourself is what is expected. You should never feel you have to be someone else to gain the friendship of another, and if you do feel this way, then perhaps it is a friendship not worth having.

3. Someone who will ***listen*** without judging you.

   One of the most underrated aspects of a friendship is the ability to listen. You should be able to do this for a friend, and your friend, in turn, should be able to do this for you. Neither of you should ever be concerned that the other will pass judgment.

4. ***Unconditional*** support.

   In good times you will have so many "friends" it will be hard to keep track. When times get tough, however, as they sometimes will, you will be able to distinguish friends from acquaintances. Unconditional support means that you do not qualify your friendships by saying: "I am your friend if . . ." There should be no "ifs" among friends.

5. Someone who will *accept* (even if they do not always understand) your choices.

   One of the more challenging aspects of a friendship is to accept the decisions and choices of friends—especially when their choices are different from the ones we would make. The issue goes back to unconditional support and being certain not to set conditions for a friendship.

6. Someone who tells you what you *need to know*, not what you want to hear.

   One of the best things friends can do for one another is to be honest with each other. Our friends should be willing to tell us the truth (regardless of how much they feel it might hurt) because in the long run it can only be beneficial.

7. A situation where you will *learn about yourself* and are a *better person* for it.

   Being honest and open with one another also means you are able to learn things about yourself that you would not know otherwise. Having greater self-awareness enables you to see your strengths and weaknesses.

Finally, your high school years will also bring peer pressure. Thus, no conversation about choosing your friends would be complete without some discussion of this topic. Peer pressure is that process in which a group of individuals attempts to force or pressure you into compromising your beliefs, values, and behavior to suit their own. Rarely does peer pressure have your best interests at heart, and yet it can be a powerful force, particularly in high school. Three very important things I learned about peer pressure and friendships in high school are as follows.

First, remember that friendship is measured not by quantity

but by quality. Few things are more precious in the world than to have true friends and to be called a true friend in return.

Second, once you give in to peer pressure, you have relinquished your freedom of choice, for if you change to suit one group, you can be certain that another group will ask you to change again. Consequently, you will become like a leaf in the wind, and whichever way the wind blows is the way you will go. You will have no control over your direction, nor will you control where you land, but you will be subject to the gusts of the wind. It is far better to be the tree whose roots go deep and who stands tall and strong regardless of the direction of the wind.

Third, remember that there are 5.2 billion people in the world and that God has given each of us our own unique set of fingerprints. No two sets are alike, and so while you may feel the pressure to be like everyone else, remember that God, in his infinite wisdom, has already made you a unique individual. No one on this planet has your walk, your talk, your style, or your smile.

Charis A. Oubre
Grambling State University, Grambling, Louisiana

Success is a degree of accomplishment, a favorable termination of a venture. Those who achieve success are on the positive road to a fulfilling life. Success is achieved only through hard work, positive role models, and an unending determination. Successful people are motivated by positive persons and profitable opportunities, much as a failure is influenced by a negative environment.

When I was younger, my friends were like me. All of us went to school and lived with a parent. We had individual personalities, of course, and distinctive hobbies, but our lifestyles were similar. Years passed and things changed. Some of my former friends quit school and began working, while others messed up by either getting pregnant or forgetting the importance of school in terms of a positive future. I was closer to those who changed for the better, mainly because we had the same goals—which the others seemed to have forgotten.

Now that I am in college, I realize that choosing friends of similar character has kept me from becoming one of those who failed. I have succeeded in graduating from high school, and I am in a higher learning setting. Yet, I have only achieved the first of many goals in life. I must continue to be influenced by positive people who will travel the same road as I. Graduating from college and receiving a master's degree—and maybe even a doctorate—are more goals that I have set for myself in order to become a complete success. Everyone should keep a goal and strive to meet it; become a success and nothing can stand in your way.

CHAPTER 11

Black Pride and Self-Esteem

VERNON L. FARMER
Associate Professor of Educational Leadership, Grambling State University, Grambling, Louisiana

During my career as a teacher in the American educational system, I have seen many African-American high school students achieving educational excellence. I marvel at their intellect, their sophistication, and their determination to succeed academically. These students have also exemplified confidence in their ability and in their commitment to achieve the immediate goal of high school graduation. Education is of course essential if we are to claim our rightful place in this nation and the world. And being successful in high school is the first of many steps we must take in making this claim.

The time you spend in high school is perhaps one of the most significant periods of your life, a period that can literally determine your future in this society. Keep in mind that a mind is a terrible thing to waste. In wasting your mind, you waste your future. Remember, education is the great equalizer, but you have the power to balance the scale of inequality.

As descendants of Africans in America, you must be educated about the achievements of African Americans to this nation. Our ancestors gave their lives to make our struggle easier, but it appears that many of us have not taken seriously the privileges that our ancestors' blood have extended to us. Therefore, as African-American high school students preparing to build for your future, and the future of your people in the twenty-first century, you must be cognizant of the great achievements of African Americans who have paved the way for you. Recognition of the contributions and experiences of these great African Americans will strengthen your pride and self-esteem and provide you with the tenacity to achieve even more than they accomplished. These great Americans not only had to dream, but also knew the right things to do to turn those dreams into reality. If you do anything less, you do a disservice to them, to my generation, to yourself, and to your children.

With this in mind, you must read about the experiences of black people in America. The literature in this area constitutes a part of the rich history of the black experience in the United States. It reveals a history of stunning accomplishments in every field of human endeavor—from literature and art to science, industry, education, diplomacy, athletics, law, and even space exploration.

Reading about these courageous African Americans will not only help you to discover the principles that you will need to guide your own lives, but also to know these black men and women in our history and to realize that the price we must pay in our struggle for equality in America is high. But you must also understand that your progress to date can in part be attributed to America's democratic system and ideals. The experiences of the African Americans you will read about in the literature are a tribute to the spirit of our democratic ideals and the system in which they have flourished.

African Americans are by nature religious. Our strong belief in God, Allah, or whatever name we choose to call the Omnipotent has been and remains the one essential fact that has guided us in our struggle for equality since we were enslaved and forcibly brought to America. The strength of our beliefs has made us one of the strongest people in the world. You must never lose sight of this fact. Never forget where you came from, what made it possible for you to get to where you are today, and what it will take to ensure your success in the future. Maintaining confidence in yourself will provide you with greater control of your destiny. You must never forget that God has given you the ability to control your destiny and that you are the navigator of your journey. You must have pride and believe in yourself and, by any means necessary, maintain your self-esteem. However, to achieve your dreams of success in high school and beyond you must ask God's guidance. God grants success to those individuals who serve him and their fellow man.

Few high schools today are homogeneous, in which all students are similar to each another in culture, race, nationality, or gender. The majority of high schools are composed of culturally diverse groups, including white Americans, African Americans, Hispanic Americans, Native Americans, Asian Americans, and mixed-race students. Nevertheless, whether you attend a high school with a homogeneous or heterogeneous student body, you will be confronted with institutionalized racism in the educational system. Sometimes groups interact, and sometimes they keep to themselves, but you are sure to encounter them in your lifetime. Learning to accept and understand people who are different from you, although many of them will not desire to understand or accept you, is an important part of expanding your global knowledge of humankind. It is this global knowledge that is part of what will make you a well-educated human being.

Division between people who are different is an all too frequent part of reality. You will almost certainly witness incidents of separatism, alienation, and isolation in your high school. For example, some students do not like others or accept them into their cliques because of cultural differences. White American students often reject others who are different or have different cognitive or learning styles than they do. Many students are threatened by these differences and choose to reject them. It can be very painful for African-American students who suffer this rejection. However, those who are on the receiving end of prejudice or discrimination must maintain their sense of pride and self-esteem in spite of racism in the society.

The literature demonstrates that the typical high school curriculum does little to change racial attitudes and behaviors toward African Americans. Consequently, many high school students, particularly white Americans, may express negative attitudes and behavior toward you and hold the pervasive stereotypes of black people. Educational policies and practices in the high school system also exemplify the negative racial beliefs and feelings of superintendents, principals, teachers, counselors, and staff. However, you cannot allow the negative attitudes, perceptions, and beliefs of these students and educators to diminish your pride and self-esteem. You must understand that self-esteem refers to self-evaluations; that is, it refers to judgments we make about our self-worth. Consequently, your subjective and personal evaluation of your ability as a student is a dominant influence as to whether you succeed or fail in high school.

If experience has taught us anything, it is that African Americans will not be able to prosper in America if they are mediocre. You must therefore utilize your education to prepare yourself for excellence. History has demonstrated that black people get an equal opportunity only when they are better than white people in a given field and endeavor. America has created its own rhetoric in opposition to affirmative action programs and has attempted to convey the notion that inept, unqualified blacks have been given jobs and opportunities to attend college at the expense of better qualified whites. However, throughout the black experience in America, blacks who have achieved academic excellence in high school and in their particular career or area of study in college have been selected as tokens and have been given opportunities that are typically available to average whites. Such practices have caused the backlash against equal opportunity for blacks. African Americans have borne a particular burden in America. We have always had to be better, with no assurance that being better would be rewarded with equal opportunities. This lack of assurance of reward should not, however, prevent you from being better and from striving to become the best. Therefore, you must work harder than ever to establish a strong academic record in high school. Having a sound high school background will provide you with the skills needed to meet the academic and career challenges you will face beyond high school.

Failure seems to be a strong fear among African-American high school students, but you can overcome it because indeed the greatest fear is fear itself. Your greatest weapon against the fear of failure is your commitment to achieve your goal. Commitment changes a dream into reality and makes the time for studying when there is no time. Success comes only with commitment, and if you fail in your attempt to achieve your goal, you can learn much from your failure. You must then regroup and try again and again, each time with an improved chance of succeeding. You must understand that experience itself can be one of the strongest confidence builders. Therefore, when you are disappointed by an outcome, maintain a positive attitude about your ability so that you can again make the challenge. You must then take the necessary steps to put everything in motion; determine what your priority goals are; motivate yourself to pursue your dreams; and maintain your commitment to your goals until you reach them. This particular path to success demands a substantial amount of energy and strength, but it tends to be effective more often than any other method. However, when you have pride and self-esteem in your ability, you will be propelled toward your goal.

Remind yourself from time to time how unique and talented you are. Learning to recognize your positive, special strengths may take time, since these strengths may not be so obvious to you initially. Some people spend their whole lives trying to build their confidence and figure out what makes them special. However, as an African-American student, you don't have the luxury of time and must move quickly to discover what makes you special. The sooner you begin the process, the better chance you will have of attaining the confidence you need to try anything you want to achieve. Even though some people will criticize you and try to dampen your spirit, you have to set the standards for yourself, retaining your confidence in your ability. Having confidence in your ability will lead to success. Tap yourself on the shoulder to show approval for your success, and console yourself when you do not succeed, convincing yourself that you will do better the next time.

You must understand, however, that you won't always fulfill your goals and expectations completely. Therefore, you must keep your eyes on the prize and always be ready to return to the drawing board to discover the source of the problem and make the appropriate adjustments. Then it will be time for you to regroup and set your sights high again with the new knowledge you have acquired.

Dealing effectively with the high school system demands a great deal of ingenuity. Your challenge as an African-American student is to discover the value that being successful in high school has for your future and the future of the African-American people and not to give up when you run into problems. Once you have discovered the value of what high school means to your life, make the most of it. You cannot afford to be dragged through or allow yourself to muddle through the educational system without making the high school experience serve your needs.

Don't waste your high school years by doing only the minimal because you will not have prepared yourselves for the challenges that lie ahead. You must take the toughest courses offered in your high school curriculum, so examine the courses offered with your guidance counselor. Do these courses include algebra and geometry? The literature demonstrates that students of all backgrounds, including African Americans, who have mastered the mathematics courses as well as courses in biology, chemistry, physics, and lab sciences, have an enormous advantage academically. Language courses, as well as courses in composition, literature, communications, and speech, are also essential to academic excellence. A strong background in mathematics will prepare you for numerous career opportunities in engineering, the sciences, business, medicine, and technology. So insist on taking these tough courses.

Although school boards, superintendents, teachers, and parents play a major role in determining the curriculum and the instruction in high school, ultimately it is you who must shoulder the major responsibility for acquiring and mastering the subject matter needed for success. Meanwhile, you will have to work hard to earn good grades when you are taking rigorous high school courses. Thorough and frequent reading, subject content tutoring, constant library visits, and participation in collaborative learning are all effective ways of mastering the subject matter.

If you work at it, studying will become routine, and soon it will be easy to see that the time devoted to adequate preparation pays off. Then you will be able to meet your academic goals and earn a competitive grade point average. African-American students can achieve excellence in high school through discipline and good study habits.

You must also read as much and as widely as you can, including newspapers, magazines, journals, novels, autobiographies, and other nonfiction literature. Also read anything else that gives you pleasure or teaches you something that you are not knowledgeable about. Taking the time to read about subjects beyond what you are assigned to read in your high school courses will make you a more informed person. When you read, you get a much broader perspective on everything.

Remember, the teacher's attitude isn't important if you know the material. It helps, however, when the teacher holds a positive view of you and believes that you have the ability to learn. Nevertheless, you must realize that a teacher's evaluation of your work can be subjective, reflecting how much she or he likes or dislikes you. Regardless of your skin color, however, the one thing that the teacher cannot take away from you is your knowledge of the subject matter. Therefore, you must make every effort to obtain absolute mastery of your courses. You will also need to take the SAT or ACT test while you are still in high school. Unfortunately, these standardized tests are not structured to measure your level of motivation, creativity, special talents, or other personal attributes. However, they are designed to test skills in vocabulary, verbal reasoning, reading comprehension, arithmetic, elementary algebra, and geometry. Therefore, if you have taken the tough high school courses and have mastered the subject matter, achieving a high score on the SAT or the ACT will not be difficult.

African Americans' ability to come as far as they have in a racist society is astounding. Although illegal, discrimination has created a strong basis for continuous progress. If this progress is to continue and we are to become a truly free people, African-American high school students must become well-educated, confident black citizens. For it is from this group that able black leaders will come and make themselves visible in every sphere of American life.

Gary Reddick
Menlo Atherton High School, East Palo Alto, California

I live in East Palo Alto, California. Until a few years ago it was a small, quiet community, but after drugs began to infiltrate the neighborhood, crime rose. Today drug dealers can be found on almost every corner. Sad to say, most of the dealers are my old schoolmates. All around me I see the results of people who have given up on education.

Fortunately for me, throughout my entire life my mother has stressed the importance of education. My mom is an African-American female who is a Stanford University graduate. I currently hold a 4.0 GPA in advanced classes, which is a result of hard work and sacrifice. I attend a school that provides me with the resources and environment needed to allow me to excel. Not every lesson, however, can be learned from a book. I was the youngest and first African-American male to be voted student body vice-president at Menlo Atherton, and I was the only freshman.

Too many youth, particularly African-American males, give up on education, but they should be aware that education and religion are the only two resources that can lead us to equality in this society. I want to get into a four-year college or university for one quite simple reason. An education will provide for me so that later I can provide for my mother, for without her there is no me.

CHAPTER 12

The Black Community: Community and Religious Involvement

JAMES COAXUM

Doctoral Candidate in Education: Focus on Administration, Planning, and Social Policy, Vanderbilt University, Nashville, Tennessee

The black church continues to be the outstanding social institution in the black community. For generations, it has served as the core around which Africans and African Americans organized their communities. For these reasons and many more, the black church has often been called the "pillar" or "cornerstone" of the black community.

Coupled with the black church, historically black colleges and universities (HBCUs) have also played a significant role in the African-American community. As stated by Blackwell, HBCUs have offered blacks a chance to achieve when no one else would; they trained more than 80 percent of all black college graduates and in the process helped develop significant leadership forces in the black community. HBCUs are still a vital component of the black community because they offer many students who might otherwise be denied admittance at other institutions the opportunity to receive postsecondary training.

In addition to the black church and HBCUs, mentors and role models also contribute to the overall success of the black community. Mentors are important for all people in all walks of life, but they are especially critical for the African-American community, standing as examples of what can be done.

In this chapter I examine the role of the black community in the lives of high school students, and more specifically, I highlight those components of the black experience that directly contribute to the success of black high school students in America. Included is a discussion of the educational roles of the religious community, historically black colleges and universities, and mentors in the lives of black high school students.

THE EDUCATIONAL ROLE OF THE RELIGIOUS COMMUNITY

The education of black Americans is rooted in the foundation of the black church. Many years ago, the door of educational opportunity was shut to black Americans. The hinges on these doors were tarnished and rusted shut with racism and hatred. The black church helped scrape away the tarnish and rust and forced those hinges to swing open. Today, you can reap the benefits from these efforts.

During the days of slavery and segregation, the black church supervised the education of its people; it was the only institution that was owned and operated solely by blacks. It was in the black church that African Americans learned the three R's—reading, writing, and arithmetic—at a time when the doors to public schools and colleges were barred by segregation. During this period, it was against the law for blacks to be educated. As a result, blacks who wanted to learn how to read and write had to do so in secret places. The black church at that time could be seen as a "Freedom Hall," but became commonly known as "The Meeting House" because it was the place where blacks could gather and be free from outside influences. It was at The Meeting House that blacks could be free to hold spiritual worship services. It was at the Freedom Hall that blacks could openly discuss matters pertaining to their well-being. In addition to offering pastoral counseling, the churches established funds within their congregation to help friends and neighbors in need; founded black colleges; and provided soup kitchens, nutritional education, housing, day care, and health care for the elderly.

The black church remains the cornerstone of the black community; however, its role in black education has taken on a new dimension. Today the primary mission of the African-American church is to "provide the cultural context that is desperately needed to enrich, support, and guide the education of black youth" (Crawford, cited in Carnegie Corporation, 1987–1988, p. 2). The role of the church has therefore changed from facilitator to enhancer. The black church adds a holistic dimension to black education, infusing programs and activities that are geared toward developing the mind, body, and spirit of young people.

By attending Sunday School classes, students strengthen their reading and comprehension skills as they are called on by teachers to read and discuss the lesson for that Sunday. Many young people in the church also develop communication skills through their participation in worship services by either reading the announcements or a scripture lesson to parishioners. They also develop leadership skills through their participation in the Youth Usher Board, the Youth Choir, or the Youth Department. Many black children first learn to read and give public speeches in the church. Regardless of whether the presentation is excellent or flawed, the audience enthusiastically receives the performance. This constantly reinforces self-esteem and pride, motivating the young people to work harder and try again.

The message of the black church for young people is always one of hope. Extra assistance with school work is often made available through tutorial and intervention programs. Black high school students often find role models and mentors in the church who encourage them to pursue postsecondary education. In many instances, these role models are the heroic figures in the success stories of students. Many churches have scholarship funds that can assist high school students during their transition to college. Above all, the black church provides a nurturing and supportive environment that enables black high school students to succeed under any circumstances.

THE ROLE OF HISTORICALLY BLACK COLLEGES AND UNIVERSITIES

HBCUs have also contributed to the success of high school students. From the beginning, controversy has surrounded the place and role of these institutions within U.S. higher education. During more than one hundred years of racial segregation and the dark period of American apartheid, HBCUs were islands of hope. These schools were established to provide higher education for blacks who by law and custom were barred from attending white private and public colleges and universities before 1954. Although the majority of black public colleges evolved when the states refused blacks admittance to existing white institutions, they are still very critical in the education of black Americans.

When selecting a college, many factors should be considered, including the community in which you will be studying. Walter Allen (1992) examined differences in the college experience between black undergraduates who attended HBCUs and those who attended predominantly white institutions (PWIs). He found that the black students attending HBCUs had higher gains than their counterparts at PWIs. The students who attended HBCUs reported better academic performance, more social involvement, and higher educational aspirations than blacks who attended PWIs. "On predominantly White campuses, Black students emphasize feelings of alienation, sensed hostility, racial discrimination, and lack of integration. On historically Black campuses, Black students emphasize feelings of engagement, connection, acceptance and extensive support and encouragement" (Allen, p. 39).

As black high school students today, you should realize the HBCUs' valuable contributions to the black community. They have produced 75 percent of the Ph.D.'s, 80 percent of the federal judges, and 85 percent of the medical doctors in the black community (Jones, 1974). HBCUs are often viewed as the training ground for leaders in the black community. The philosophy of these institutions is that everyone can learn and therefore accept ordinary (or marginal) high school students and turn them into extraordinary scholars. Through strong relationships with faculty, staff, and peers, you have the opportunity to maximize your potential and go on to great accomplishments. HBCUs also offer the opportunity for you to enhance your leadership skills. Because most students at HBCUs do not feel a sense of isolation, but rather a sense of connectedness, they are able to spend more time on academic issues.

Historically black colleges and universities play a vital role in the black community and in the system of postsecondary education. College students perform better intellectually and are socially more integrated in an environment where they feel comfortable (Lang, 1994). As a result, when thinking about college choice, you should spend time answering the following questions, as set forth by Lang: "Where will I be most comfortable socially and intellectually? Where can I succeed and accomplish what it is I want to accomplish from my college experience? And where can I best adapt to the surrounding environment and have the best opportunity for personal success?"

THE ROLE OF MENTORS AND ROLE MODELS

The term *mentor* has been defined and described by many scholars seeking to understand the fundamentals of this phenomenon. Words often associated with the term include *guide, sponsor, facilitator, supporter,* and *big brother/sister.* Mentors and role models are important in the lives of high school students because they have the power to facilitate dreams and make them reality. Finding a mentor can be one of the most important actions of your high school years. Students with mentors have a far greater advantage than those who do not because they usually make a rough transition smoother. Mentors usually work from within a system to bring an outside person into the same system. This is usually done through a mentor's informal contacts or by a mentor providing insights to the outside person. For example, a high school senior interested in attending Morehouse College could benefit from having a student already enrolled in the college as his or her mentor. The mentor who works from inside the system could provide hints that would make for a stronger application or speak on the person's behalf to members of the admissions committee. Certainly, the high school student may enhance his or her chance of being admitted, more so than his or her friend who is also interested but has no mentor at the college. High school students should develop relationships with persons who could facilitate their growth.

Although many mentors and role models in the black community are found in churches and HBCUs, not all students participate in religious institutions or know persons associated with black colleges. This is particularly true for urban students whose communities are depicted as economically deprived. Do these students have the opportunity to cultivate relationships with those who can assist them? Yes, many mentors and role models reside in the communities with these students. Such a mentor is sometimes known as the "local hero." Everyone in the community knows of this person, and if the community were polled, many would point to this person as a role model.

Within the black community, there are social institutions known as community centers. They are located in the heart of the community and serve as the hub for families residing in the area. These centers serve as an extended family network to community residents, offering workshops, seminars, and activities that are geared toward improving the quality of life. These community centers are staffed with volunteer mentors who tutor students and encourage them to work to their fullest potential. These centers also offer extracurricular activities such as basketball teams to keep young people occupied and off the streets.

Community centers instill self-esteem and ethnic pride. Through after-school and rites of passage programs, students obtain a greater sense of identity and begin to decide where they will fit into the society. These centers have given high school students much of what they needed to make it to and through college. When many successful students are asked how they beat the odds, they answer that someone believing in them—a mentor, a role model, a program leader—made the difference. Thus, mentors and role models are a vital part of any community and play a major role in the success of young people residing in that community.

The old African proverb, "It takes a whole village to raise a child," expresses a philosophy to which the black community has always subscribed. Even in this era when black families continue to reap the harsh brutalities of slavery, the "village" is coming together to save the young. Black churches today more than ever are concerned with the plight of their youth. Churches are opening their doors not only on Sunday mornings, but also throughout the week, providing youth, even non-members, a positive alternative.

Historically black colleges and universities are members of the village, serving as the gateway to higher educational opportunity. For many black high school graduates, HBCUs provide the access that enables students to compete for jobs in the "real world." Black community centers primarily serve those young people living in urban areas, but like the black church, provide programs and activities that send a message of hope. These centers act as extended families in the village, providing support systems for those young persons who are not part of a religious denomination or lack support from the home.

Mentors and role models, the underlying force that allows the village to raise successful high school students, are known as dream makers and hope givers. They encourage young people to dream, and they facilitate the process that may make those dreams a reality. The black community's role in the success of black high school students then is to ensure that all students are reached by some aspect of the village.

The black church, historically black colleges and universities, community centers, and mentors are all essential components of the village. They have nurtured and raised many generations of black children, and they continue to serve as the primary foundation on which dreams are cultivated in the black community. The interrelated activities of these social institutions foster self-esteem and ethnic pride in young people and make it possible for black high school students to become successful. You should keep these concepts in mind as you begin to mold your academic and career paths. Being a well-rounded individual and keeping involved with various activities are crucial in broadening your opportunities for success.

REFERENCES

Allen, W. R. (1992). "The Color of Success: African American College Student Outcomes at Predominantly White and Historically Black Public Colleges and Universities." *Harvard Educational Review* 62 (1): 26–43.

Carnegie Corporation of New York. (1987–1988). "Black Churches: Can They Strengthen the Black Family?" *Carnegie Quarterly* 33 (2): 1–9.

Jones, B. A. (1974). "The Tradition of Sociology Teaching in Black Colleges: The Unheralded Profession." In J. E. Blackwell and

M. Janowitz, eds., *Black Sociologists* (pp. 121–163). Chicago: University of Chicago Press.

Lang, M. (1994). "Should I Choose a Black College or an Integrated College?" In R. D. Higgins, C. B. Cook, W. J. Ekeler, R. M. Sawyer, and K. W. Prichard, eds., *The Black Student's Guide to College Success* (pp. 9–15). Westport, Conn.: Greenwood Press.

Laura Cole
Wellesley College, Wellesley, Massachusetts

During high school I often contemplated the safest and most legitimate ways of escaping the clustered two-bedroom apartment in Brooklyn where I lived, my strong-tempered brother, and an array of other confrontations that encouraged mischief. By observing the actions of the people in my environment, I subtly figured out that being truant, becoming pregnant, or using drugs were paths I should definitely not follow. In conclusion, I decided that college would be the ideal solution for my situation because it would give me the opportunity to be independent and gain useful knowledge for my future. This plan helped me to view my education as an investment and motivated me to do whatever was necessary to get to college. I tried to define my goals clearly so that I could actively think of methods to achieve them. Since I was making this major effort, I aimed for the top colleges, well aware that they were only accepting quality students. Working hard to receive high grades and getting involved in extracurricular activities would have to be a priority in order to ensure my goal of success. Success, as I defined it in this context, meant effort and college-level academic quality. With that in mind, I completed high school six months early with academic honors.

While college was a means of escaping a frustrating home life, it was only one source of motivation for achieving in high school. Although college is no guarantee for life success, I believed, and still do believe, that education is the passport to life chances, especially for minorities. I was fortunate to encounter teachers and friends with similar values who encouraged me in a positive direction. Having a variety of extended conversations in the fourth floor hallway with Mr. Schneider, my eleventh grade mathematics teacher, about the experiences of his college-age children, the latest reactions to the Rodney King verdict, or my own concerns for financial security helped me to nurture my thinking as a unique individual. His friendship and affirmations were a great reward to me. My mother's involvement in my academic life also influenced me enormously because she helped me establish high standards for success that were realistic. I wanted to get high grades not only because my friends were getting them, but also because achievement was valued as something positive, not something corny. These values and standards guided my actions; "failure" was not an option because I knew I was capable of succeeding at almost anything with enough effort. If I did "fail," I tried to view it as a learning experience in order to prevent the same mistake twice. I would have made many more mistakes, terrible ones, without help from my mother, teachers, and friends. My high school experience and my life in general are positive because of the strong, dependable support system they provided. I think I am justified, however, in patting myself on the back for making the choice to utilize these human resources.

The transition from high school to college was not easy. Attending college has been one of the most difficult, yet gratifying, experiences in my life. While the college environment has allowed me to reinforce and develop skills and ideals that I held previously, it has also challenged me to question myself. It is through this process that I have matured the most in skill and sensitivity. If I did not question myself during high school, making conscious decisions to diligently complete homework and stay off the streets, I would not be a content stressed-out sophomore at Wellesley College asking myself new and challenging questions. Being able to evaluate myself, define goals, actively work toward these goals, and ask for help when I needed it is how I made it through high school and on to college. Most critically, being aware of both my strengths and weaknesses gave me the knowledge and confidence to persevere. Although I often feel drained from the rigors of academia, and my life just seems very hectic, my education continues to be the one thing I have the most control over. My education has enhanced my ability to help myself to succeed. We all possess this innate power if we choose to recognize it.

CHAPTER 13

Integration with Others

LAWANNA GUNN-WILLIAMS

Chair, Department of Sociology and Psychology, Grambling State University, Grambling, Louisiana

Philosophically, the United States is a country that provides equal education for all its public school children. But for many of those left out of the socioeconomic and cultural mainstream, equality in education remains elusive. Unlike what many people think, equality—equal rights and equal treatment for all—is not just the product of the leadership of teachers and administrators within the school. Equality also entails self-acceptance, self-involvement, and integration with others.

Many African-American youth find themselves socially and emotionally isolated within the constraints of their high school walls because of low self-esteem, feelings of inadequacy, or social rejection. Such negative feelings are the result of a history of slavery, degradation, and segregation. However, to receive the full benefits of the high school educational experience, these students must refrain from thinking negatively about self and others, for negative thoughts promote hostility and social withdrawal and often limit the degree of integration with others.

Becoming involved is one way in which the African-American high school student can integrate with others, forming friendships, associations, and social networks. Integrating with others is not easy, however. Integration implies developing relationships in which the student feels genuinely involved. Most adolescents enter high school having had few quality social relationships with persons outside of their families, neighborhood friends, and school peers. Initial integration with people from various communities and groups can therefore be awkward. Yet, the benefits of integrating certainly outweigh any associated difficulties or discomforts.

BENEFITS OF INTEGRATING

When the high school student becomes an active participant in social relationships with peers and school personnel, the quality of the student's school experiences begins to increase. Through interaction with others, he or she comes to an understanding of different viewpoints and establishes a variety of goals. Hence, this experience broadens horizons. Integration with others also brings about a sense of "oneness" that arises from the student's developing feeling of acceptance. This sense of security is generally reflected in the student's grades, social behavior, and personal disposition, all of which improve.

STEPS IN INTEGRATING WITH OTHERS

If properly followed, the procedures involved in the integration process as outlined here will protect the student's individuality, as well as facilitate the integration process.

Step 1: Be Confident

Being confident implies having faith or trust in yourself. People who are self-confident have a sense of self-worth. They are able to see a future for themselves, for they trust in their own capabilities. The high school student who is self-confident is less likely to become involved in crime or drug abuse. This student feels good about self and others and is likely to have high ambitions in life, because confidence perpetuates a desire to achieve.

In order to achieve a sense of self-confidence, you must accept and love yourself. And in order to love yourself, you must know yourself; you must know what you value, like, and dislike. With self-knowledge, you know what is important in life, and you are able to understand your own talents and abilities. If you take a close look at past experiences and at the particular people who have been a part of your life experiences, you can learn much about yourself. Our associations indicate many value choices and preferences.

Once you know yourself, you can give yourself a stamp of approval or disapproval. If you find that you possess certain traits that you do not like, actively work to change them.

Step 2: Choose Your Friends Wisely

Bad company can destroy a student. Ideally, you should integrate with friends who can help you grow as an individual. Do not give in to peer pressure from people who exhibit unacceptable behavior. This type of integration is detrimental.

If you feel good about yourself, you will be able to ignore the rebellious crowd and stay out of the fast lane. The individual with a sense of self-worth is more selective in the choice of friends and acquaintances. Your integration with others will generally involve those who support you in your goals and ambitions. People with similar outlooks on life tend to associate with each other.

Reach out to those persons with similar ideas and values. Do not select your friends on the basis of racial, ethnic, or socioeconomic group affiliation. True friendship knows no color and no monetary value. Associate with those who can help you achieve your goals, simply because they, too, are striving to achieve in life. Seek positive friends who critique and challenge you. Take an interest in their activities and encourage them to work jointly on some school assignments or activities with you. You will be surprised at the number of friends you can make in a short period of time.

Know your friends and accept their limitations. No one is perfect, so you can expect occasional disappointments, and they in turn, at some time, will no doubt be disappointed by your behavior. Friendship is a golden commodity and is not to be discarded simply because a person fails to meet certain of your expectations. We all have weak spots in our character; it is the responsibility of a true friend to point out that weak spot and help to strengthen it where possible.

A young professional man, Chuck, had many friends from all walks of life. One of Chuck's friends, Leo, was quite his opposite. While Chuck was very professional, Leo was quite unprofessional. Chuck was well polished and formal in his interactions with others, whereas Leo was unpolished and crude. Chuck was a man of his word, but Leo would often exaggerate the truth and even blatantly lie. When asked why they continued to be friends, Chuck replied, "One thing I have learned in life is that true friends are not easy to find. I value my friendships, but I also make sure that I know my friends. There are certain friends whom I trust with certain responsibilities or with particular areas in which they are strong. Knowing the vulnerabilities of my friends allows me to protect myself from being disappointed by them and still receive the benefits of our relationships."

Know your friends and associate with them in ways that enhance their strong points, and be a source of strength to them where they are weak. Set a positive example and do not allow their vulnerabilities to weaken you.

Step 3: Set Goals and Pursue Them

Les Brown is one of America's greatest public speakers, an author, as well as a rising television star. In his book *Live Your Dreams*, Les describes a childhood experience in which some of his richer friends offered him a ride home after a high school play one night. Being too embarrassed to have them let him out at his own little shotgun house in a lower class neighborhood, he told them that he lived across town, and he led them to a beautiful mansion that he had always admired. The mansion was a doctor's home, and Les always dreamed that he would have a house like it someday.

When the friends dropped him off, they were quite impressed by the beautiful mansion. Les thought that they would simply let him out and leave, but they did not. Instead, they told him that they would wait until he was safely inside and blinked the lights. Les thought hurriedly of what he would have to do. He told his friends to go on, because he had to walk around the back to get the hidden key. Finally, they drove away, but Les walked slowly toward the house in case they decided to circle the block. As soon as he was sure that his friends were out of sight, Les ran like mad to the bus station to get a ride home.

The next day at school, his friends told others that "Les Brown lives in a mansion." He thought, "Not yet, but one day I will" (Brown, 1992). Today Les Brown does indeed live in a mansion. He had a dream, he set his goals, and he pursued them. If you actively pursue your goals and never let go of your dreams, they may well become realities.

Step 4: Be a Humanitarian

Have a genuine love in your heart for people. Individuals who sincerely love others are generally loved by others. Love breeds love.

After her father was transferred because of his job, Tammy, a junior in high school, had to leave her home in Chicago and move to Louisiana with her family. She had been devastated upon learning that she would have to leave Southside High, where she had made many friends, and graduate from a school in a strange city.

As the family's van made its southbound voyage, Tammy quietly wept. She thought of her friends at Southside High and of all the fun they had had through the years. Then, suddenly, she thought back on how apprehensive she had been upon entering ninth grade. Leaving junior high was an unsettling experience for her because she had to say goodbye to many of her peers, never to see them again. Yet, entering high school had been made easier by her father's advice: "If you are a friend to others, others will be friends to you." And so she again drew from his wise counsel as she entered Eastside High in Louisiana. She came to school her first day armed with a smile on her face, and through her loving heart, she easily won the hearts of others. Tammy consistently and sincerely showed love, respect, and concern for everyone in her school environment, and, by the end of the school year, to no one's surprise, she was unanimously named "Miss Eastside High."

Showing love for others reflects our love for ourselves. Love, much as is true of a smile, is contagious. Love others not because of what they can do for you or because of who they are, but in spite of their differences and in spite of their limitations. Love is the most powerful force we can exercise to integrate with others. It helps us to ignore the petty differences dividing us, and it helps us to accept each other.

You can successfully integrate with others on the high school campus by maintaining a positive sense of self. Self-esteem frees us to assume active roles in meaningful relationships by sharing our ideas and beliefs without losing our own individuality.

Integration with others in school will likely produce a positive change in your academic work and personal life. Integration with others is essential not only in high school but throughout life. Your success in life and your happiness in life depend, to a great degree, on your ability to integrate. The successful high school student will be the integrating high school student.

REFERENCES

Brown, L. *Live Your Dreams*. (1992). New York: William Morrow and Co.

Comer, J. P., and A. F. Poussaint. (1992). *Raising Black Children*. New York: Penguin Books.

Edelman, M. W. (1992). *The Measure of Our Success*. Boston: Beacon Press.

Sedlacek, W. E., and G. C. Brooks. (1976). *Racism in American Education: A Model for Change*. Chicago: Nelson Hall.

ShaShawn Covington
Whites Creek High School, Nashville, Tennessee

In today's society, high school teenagers need positive forces in their lives, people who are willing to help steer them away from negative influences such as gang violence, drug abuse, and teenage pregnancy. In my life, I have always had positive influences who provided a listening ear and encouraging words just when I needed them most. These positive influences, often called mentors, along with my family, church, and community, have made the difference in my life.

As I reflect on my high school years, I find that many people played a role in my success. The most important influence on my life is my physician and friend, Dr. Comelia Graves. Dr. Graves, affectionately known as Connie, is an Ob/Gyn who specializes in high-risk pregnancy cases at the Vanderbilt University Medical Center. She has been an advocate for me throughout my high school years. In addition to helping me prepare for exams and get out my college applications, she has often provided that listening ear when I experienced negative peer pressure.

My mother, Sandra Covington, and my grandmother, Claretha Branch, have also contributed to my success in high school. In addition to being the two strongest black female figures in my life, during my childhood years these women instilled in me the unflagging desire for excellence. They taught me that success begins with *me* and that to fail is not to try. They have taught me how to have pride in myself, and how to "hold fast to dreams."

The community and my local church have also been important to my development. As a high school senior, I had the opportunity to participate with the INROADS/Nashville Program, an organization that helps high school students in the Nashville area secure internships in the fields of business and engineering. The program has proved to be an enriching experience for me. Through our Saturday meetings, I have been able to enhance my speaking, writing, and math skills. I have also had the opportunity to visit several college campuses, including Tennessee State, Middle Tennessee State University, and the University of Tennessee at Knoxville.

I am a member of Payne Chapel African Methodist Episcopal Church in Nashville, a church that offers a wonderful array of activities geared to young people. I am also a member of the Youth Mass Choir, the Sister Love Mentoring Program, and the Young People and Children's Division, and I have participated as a volunteer with the Living Breadbox Ministry. All of these organizations are positive alternatives to the street. They are staffed with committed adults who take the plight of African-American children seriously. Participating with youth-oriented organizations at my local church has given me the rare opportunity to interact with other young people who are serious about their future.

All of my experiences have converged to make me humble, enthusiastic, and excited about every new possibility that comes my way. The black community has certainly had an impact on my life. Most importantly, it has provided me with mentors, role models, and coaches who stand on my sideline cheering, supporting, and encouraging me to reach for the stars.

CHAPTER 14

Part-time Work: An Education and Opportunity

AL B. BARRON

Director, Career Counseling and Placement Center, Southern University, Baton Rouge, Louisiana

Career opportunities for young African Americans entering the workforce have never been as exciting as they are today, and the best way to start that career is through part-time employment, especially if you are in high school. This will give you an opportunity to see what the world of work is all about.

Employers are looking for certain characteristics in a part-time employee. Namely, they want (1) someone who is clean, well groomed, speaks intelligently, and wears clothes neatly (not oversized or backward) and (2) someone who is going to be dependable, at work on time, and not necessarily the first one to leave. Those are the characteristics that excite an employer, and you have to show your eagerness to learn and to get started in this thing called the world of work.

Part-time employment means the jobs at your corner grocery stores, your local McDonald's, or maybe even your own small business, such as cutting grass. In this type of employment there is a system in place in which everybody has a job to do and is held responsible for doing it. In these jobs you gain knowledge that will help you later in life. Employers like to see these types of part-time jobs on your resume because it shows that you have gone through the system.

Every job is a good job and should be listed on your resume, even if it is only baby-sitting. Having a baby-sitting job shows you have human relations skills, that you are responsible enough to follow instructions, and that you are reliable and dependable.

Getting a part-time job also means you are taking the time to investigate what type of work or career you would like to pursue when you are an adult. How do you do that? You can investigate careers through the Internet or by talking to people who are doing the things you would like to do. For instance, if you are interested in being a nurse, you can contact home health agencies and ask whether they offer part-time opportunities for students. This will put you in contact with people who are doing what you want to do in life. If you are interested in accounting, for example, talk to accountants who are doing the things you would like to do. It is also important for you to see the educational side of the job that you are considering. So to be an accountant you will learn that you need to take math classes. Seeing people doing what you want to do will give you a tremendous feeling of excitement, of "Hey! I can do that!"

All over the country programs have been set up to encourage young people to get involved in various careers. One of the best programs available today is the Black Achievers Program, which has been set up in the YMCA with professionals from all disciplines and walks of life. These professionals work with young people, guiding them not only to part-time jobs, but also to careers they may never have considered on their own.

Part-time employment can help you pinpoint your area of interest, without locking you into any field. The Bureau of Labor Statistics points out that before you finally retire you will probably change jobs seven times and your career maybe three times. The Bureau of Labor Statistics Workforce 2000 report also reveals that one out of every three persons in the workforce will either be a minority or a female. That is an overwhelming statistic. So there are going to be plenty of jobs for those who are technically prepared for these jobs. The great thing about part-time employment is that it will enable you to investigate what you would like to do careerwise.

Above all, you should adjust yourself to change: Be ready for it, accept it, and know it is going to happen. Change is everywhere, and you have to be ready for it. It is therefore important to get a good education to get your background and your studies together. In this way, you will be able to move from one career to another. A part-time job will give you an opportunity to investigate your options. Is this really what I want to do? But remember your first job is not your last job. If you are constantly late for work, you will be labeled undependable. You have got to be on time, and you've got to be there to do your job effectively.

In part-time employment, you must be able to work with others. You must investigate what it is you want to do, and you must be able to take suggestions from others. When you go to college, you will soon decide on your major. Whatever you decide, make sure it's *your* decision and not that of your friends. The road to success is difficult, and it is traveled with a lot of people. But *you* have to determine which road you want to take; your friends may not be with you, and so you will have to determine that on your own You alone have to discover how big your dream is.

A part-time job is a great indicator of what type of worker you are going to be. In this unique learning experience, you will find out how you match up with others. Your employer will soon let you know if you are not doing a good job and will give you constructive criticism on what you should be doing. The workplace is not a place to socialize; you must go there and be ready to work. That's what it is all about!

When you begin to look for work, make sure first that you

seek out the Junior Achievement and other businesses in the area and ask them for a part-time job that can turn into a career opportunity or business. It is easier to see yourself as successful when you talk to successful people. Indeed, you need to surround yourself with positive thinking people, people who look like you and people who are doing what you would like to do. You have got to see that you have the opportunity to be as big as you want to be. You must dream big or don't dream at all. You've also got to take a serious look at yourself. The hardest thing you must do is find out what your dream is; then you must educate yourself to make your dream a reality.

Each point is a stepping stone to the other. Thus, those of you who are looking at the next six years as being a great time in your life are the individuals who are willing to sacrifice and pay the price to accomplish your dreams. If you are reading this book, you are halfway there; you must also keep yourself abreast of what is going on in the workforce. You are going to school to become educated so that you can learn various skills, and go into the workplace or the job market and sell yourself. It is as if you are a product, and you are marketing yourself for sale.

You must stay drug free! Drugs are part of society, and once you get a job, you may be tested for drugs. So again I counsel you to be accountable. If you say you are going to be somewhere, you must be there and not make excuses. A football coach once told me that excuses only satisfy those who make them, a statement I have found to be very true. Sure you're going to make mistakes—that is how we all learn—but you must learn from your mistakes and not make the same ones over and over.

That part-time job that you think is not important right now will pay off later. It can be used as a reference to help you secure your next job. Along with the money you will make, it will also teach you some valuable lessons about life. Earning your own money will allow you to pay for those Jordan's that cost $130. Even better, if you're spending your own money, you may not even buy those Jordan's because you worked hard for your money and you figure that maybe Mike's got enough money already and he may not need your $130. You make better decisions once you start making your own money. That's what I like about kids getting a part-time job—they can see how tough it is to earn money. Once you start making your own money, you begin making informed decisions.

As a young man, I can remember cutting grass, washing cars, and helping electricians and painters. None of those part-time jobs ended up as my career, but they encouraged some strong values in me, such as being on time, being honest and truthful with people, and being the best person I can be. Martin Luther King, Jr., said it best when he said if you are a street sweeper, sweep streets like Michelangelo painted the Sistine Chapel. You have got to strive to be the best you can be and take pride in your work.

If you ever have the opportunity to be mentored in business by one of your city's great business leaders, take that as a blessing from God and soak up as much information as you possibly can. Take advantage of every opportunity that comes to you. As I said in the beginning, this is the most exciting time to be young and entering the workforce. Be sure to explore the opportunities of part-time employment and work to become the best you can be.

Stacie LaCresha Mitchell-Ole-Sabay
Graduate, North High School, Des Moines, Iowa

As an African-American female, I consider myself a successful student in the pursuit of my high school education. In my high school years, I set goals for myself, strove for excellence, and upheld my dignity.

I am a graduate of North High School in Des Moines, Iowa. My years in high school were not easy, for I faced a lot of the challenges that young African-American students are experiencing even today. However, with the grace of God I can say today that nothing is impossible. Peer pressure was among my most critical challenges. I had some friends with goals and others who were discouraging, and yet I never lost my desire to move forward.

Fortunately, I was able to acknowledge my identity. I understood that my life had a purpose, and I appreciated my potential, seeking to invest in it despite any limitations. I knew that with the will of God success was in my hands. Even though I lived in an unconducive environment, I succeeded because I had a positive attitude.

I had personal esteem and trusted in my capabilities, relying on God's power. I was also focused. I knew the struggle was tough, and yet I had a vivid hope that through Jesus Christ who strengthens me I could do all things. I never faltered or gave up.

My education was successful in part because I was willing to share and to help others. Whatever I wished for myself I also wanted for others. Even though I had a lot to do for myself, I was never too tired to volunteer in programs that helped others in school, the community, the church, and my own family.

I would like to encourage all my dear brothers and sisters who are pursuing a high school education. Hold on to your goals and remain positive at all cost. If you invest in helping your community, you will reap the best and enjoy life, remembering that the beginning of success is fear of God and rejection of evil.

Finally, we need to redefine our freedom so that our individual freedom will not collide with other people's interests. We must understand that our freedom is simply to do what is right, and that rather than dwell on the past we should learn from it. We should also strive to appreciate life rather than complain about it. Keep in mind that *no* weapon formed against us shall prosper. Be positive.

In memory of my father Roylee Whitfield

CHAPTER 15

The Career Hunt: Putting It All Together

DEREN FINKS

Director of Admissions, Harvey Mudd College, Claremont, California

One of life's greatest satisfactions is having a profession you enjoy, for, after all, we usually end up spending more time at work than at home. Getting up and going to a job you enjoy can be a key to overall satisfaction and happiness in life. So, finding the right career is an important part of growing up and becoming independent.

Believe it or not, most people find their professions by accident. For some, this has worked and for others it has not. Having a well-laid-out plan for finding your eventual occupation will not guarantee satisfaction, but like most things in life, it will increase the odds that your career choice will be a good match for you. Three areas are part of any well-planned career hunt: exploration, preparation, and action.

EXPLORATION

What do you want to do? This is a seemingly simple question, but for most people it's very difficult to answer because there are so many choices out there. One of the best ways to determine your career is to go to college. Usually, the more interesting and well-paying professions require some kind of higher education—sometimes only a four-year bachelor's degree is needed, while other careers require several years of graduate study. In many cases, your major in college is not important; what is important is that you've earned the degree. College is a wonderful place to try many different subjects in order to find out what you really enjoy. While attending a college or university, you will be exposed to a variety of majors and possible careers. Nearly every college has a career planning and placement office that can help you determine which graduate schools you should consider or which jobs you might want to think about. Once you have completed your studies, the career planning and placement office can also help you with resume writing, interview skills, and leads on position openings. In order to prepare for college, you should take the most challenging courses you can manage and do well in them. There is a college or university for just about anyone who wants to attend. However, the more successful you are in your studies, the more choices of careers you'll have. This is one reason why grades are so important.

With our rapidly changing technology and societal needs, some of the choices you have today may be obsolete tomorrow. By the same token, some of the career choices you may have later have not yet been born. So making a definite career decision at this stage is not important. What is important is that you take a thorough look at yourself to determine your strengths, weaknesses, and desires. With this information in hand, you can begin to determine which opportunities to consider.

Self-assessment is not as easy as you may think. You will

have to ask yourself some thoughtful questions. Here are a few examples:

1. Do you enjoy working with the public? Do you enjoy working with people in general?

2. Are you detail oriented? Are you highly organized?

3. What is your personality type? Outgoing? Shy? Would you prefer to be in the forefront or behind the scenes?

The toughest part of doing this exercise is coming up with honest answers. You have to answer these types of questions based on the character traits that describe *who you are* and not *who you want to be*. That's not to say you can't change or build on the attributes you wish to improve, but you want to be careful to avoid a career that doesn't match your personal style. For example, if you know you are a notorious procrastinator, then a position that demands meeting rigid daily or weekly deadlines is probably not for you. Similarly, if you have an outgoing and gregarious personality, and you like being the center of attention, you should probably stay away from careers that require you to spend most of your day in front of a computer terminal. The key is to find an occupation that will allow you to utilize your dominant personal characteristics.

Based on your self-assessment, you should look around you to see what kinds of professions are out there. Of course, family, friends, and acquaintances will usually talk with you about what they do; this is always a good beginning. When you talk to them, however, you should not only be curious about what positions they hold, but should also ask about the people with whom they work. Sometimes you may find that their bosses or the employees they supervise have much more interesting jobs.

After you've surveyed your relatives, you may be feeling confident enough to go out on your own to look at different types of careers. As you go through everyday life, you may discover other interesting jobs. Whether you go to the shopping mall or visit a museum, you're in some way experiencing someone's hard work. Some of these occupations are obvious: department managers, buyers, architects, fashion designers, window dressers, artists, docents, or curators. But others require you to think a little more. Who decides which colors of plants or types of flowers to plant outside the building to make sure it looks appealing? The landscape architect. Who decides to hang the colorful banners from the high ceiling in the mall to give it a cheerful appearance? The industrial interior designer. Who decides how long this particular museum exhibit will be shown? The museum program manager. Who traveled to Peru to make sure these rare artifacts were transported safely to this museum? The museum collections manager. And so on.

Many people find the idea of being a professional entertainer or athlete to be attractive, but not many people have the talent and also the luck to get these jobs. So, most people become disappointed and give up. But it's important to be aware that these fields offer other career opportunities that are most fulfilling. The stage managers, production managers, set designers, casting agents, and wardrobe managers have great jobs as do the sports agents, scouts, trainers, team managers, and public relations staffs.

Once you find several professions that are of interest to you, it's a good idea to conduct career interviews. One of the things I've learned over the years is that people who like their jobs enjoy talking about them. It's very flattering when someone takes an interest in what you do. So, when you find a career that interests you, try to talk with someone who is involved in that kind of work. If you are patient with his or her schedule and if you are professional in your demeanor, doing career interviews will provide some great experiences. First, however, you should find out everything you can about the profession you plan to investigate. Doing an information search in a good library is an excellent start. You may wish to browse through trade magazines or newsletters that cover topics and issues relating to specific occupations. This will familiarize you with any terms or background information you may need in order to conduct a successful interview. Next, you should set up an appointment to talk with someone who does the kind of work you find interesting. Usually, this is as easy as picking up the phone and calling the individual or organization and explaining what you want to do. You may have to call several companies if the first ones are unable to help you. If you're contacting an individual, however, you need to be mindful of your interviewee's accessibility. For example, if you're thinking about becoming a professional actor, I doubt you would be very successful gaining an interview with Denzel Washington! But there are almost always professional regional or community theaters where you'll find actors and actresses happy to talk to you about their profession. Regardless of what type of career interests you, here are some basic questions you may wish to ask in a career interview:

1. How did you decide to do this kind of work? What other jobs have you had in the past that prepared you for or led you to this one?

2. What do you like about your career? What's your least favorite part?

3. What personality traits are most helpful in doing this kind of work?

4. What training or educational background is helpful in becoming successful in your career? Are there specific areas in which I should concentrate in college? Is having a graduate degree helpful in your profession?

5. To advance in your career, what would be the next step for you? How long does advancement generally take, and what do you have to do to prepare for it?

6. What advice could you give me about how to prepare for a career in your field?

After the interview experience, *always* mail the person whom you interviewed a thank-you note. If there was a secretary or someone else you found helpful in setting up your meeting, you should send a note to him or her as well. Often the people you meet will have to put something else aside to make time for you, so be sure to show your appreciation.

PREPARATION

The time to start preparing for your future college and career is in high school. All the things you do now will have an impact on your life. Your extracurricular activities, the classes you choose, and the grades you get can impact which college you attend or the jobs for which you'll be considered.

The best way to prepare yourself for the future is to be broad-based in all of your choices. Today more than ever it's important that you have a variety of experiences and a solid base of knowledge. Because the opportunities available are always changing, today's students need a multitude of skills. So, the best way for you to prepare yourself for the job market is to concentrate on gaining strong, basic skills that are transferrable to a variety of professions. No matter what profession you choose, higher education is *always* a benefit. Well-honed skills in writing, mathematics, critical thinking, organization, leadership, and management of projects and people is imperative. The courses you choose in high school and in college should be broad in scope and include a wide variety of subjects.

Most students don't realize that taking an English class in which you have to interpret novels or poems teaches you to think analytically and will provide you with the skills necessary to solve problems in the workplace. Studying a foreign language or having strong skills in mathematics also helps in developing these skills. In fact, in all the classes you've had or will have in school, sometimes the thinking process you develop is just as important as, if not more important than, the subject matter itself. But keep in mind that few people have become successful without some background in mathematics, literature, history, government, politics, and all the other subjects you may study.

Your extracurricular activities are also great places to learn skills that will be valuable in most professions. Working on the yearbook staff or school newspaper, for example, will help you learn to become organized and develop marketable managerial skills. Being involved in student government or working on the homecoming committee teaches you leadership and how to work with all kinds of people. Playing competitive sports teaches you the value of cooperation and teamwork. Keeping your experiences broad-based will help prepare you for a work world that is constantly changing. Furthermore, this work world demands that employees have a great deal of flexibility in their area of expertise.

As you begin to progress through your career plan, you should look for a person who could be your mentor. A mentor can point you in the direction of a career that may be of interest to you, help you find the best college or university, advise you on your life issues, or even be a "sounding board" to give you feedback on your ideas. Your mentor could be a teacher or counselor at your school, a neighbor, or a mature friend or mature relative who is successful, wise, and interested in seeing you succeed. Your mentor should also be someone you trust and feel you can speak with openly. Throughout your life you may have several mentors: a counselor from high school, a professor at college, a co-worker or even a relative. It is always important that you have access to a knowledgeable person who can help you find the right path to success.

ACTION

Once you've narrowed your interests to a few specific areas, you should begin taking some concrete steps toward resume building through course work, internships, and networking. When employers look to fill vacant positions, they sometimes comb through hundreds of resumes to find only a few candidates they want to interview. Consequently, the resume you submit for employment is your only chance to show you are qualified for a position. Building your resume to suit the field you wish to pursue is an important task.

If through your exploration you find that the profession you want to pursue requires a specific college degree (i.e., engineering, architecture) or academic courses in certain areas (i.e., nursing, medicine), then you should take steps as early as possible to satisfy these requirements. Always make sure you rely on the appropriate school or college staff members to advise you in selecting the proper course of study. You may also wish to contact the business in which you're interested for advice on the best way to prepare for a career in their organization.

No matter what your chosen career path, one of the best ways to show your preparedness is to obtain direct experience in the field you plan to pursue. Part-time work, internships, or apprenticeships are excellent ways of getting a background in your chosen career. Often, companies have positions available for students who wish to know more about the type of work they do. Internships are sometimes paid but are most often volunteer positions. Through your high school or college placement office, or even on your own, contact companies whose business is related to the field you plan to enter. Ask whether internships or apprenticeships are available. If no paid internships are available, ask to volunteer. Later, if the company finds your hard work valuable, it may create a paid position for you. But remember, it's the experience that is most valuable to you—not the money. Either way, you will come away with direct experience in the profession, and you will know people who are familiar with the quality of your work. These are people you can rely on as references or to provide letters of recommendation on your behalf.

Getting to know people who can help you find a position in your field of choice is an important part of the career hunt. When looking for a position, it's important to be in touch with anyone who may have insight, contacts, or influence. This is called networking. Through part-time jobs, internships, professors, family, friends, and acquaintances you will often find leads on jobs that can be important stepping stones to a rewarding career.

These are only a few steps on how to progress through the career hunt. There are many pathways to success, and you should feel free to experiment with various methods. Hopefully, however, this chapter has provided you with a basic framework to get you started in the right direction toward a rewarding profession.

Christopher Tyler
Sultan Senior High School, Sultan, Washington

I have always had an interest in how things work and in how I can build things to work on my own. In my spare time, I enjoy tinkering with chemicals or electronic devices in the hopes of creating something (i.e., fireworks or radios) out of the supplies at hand. My particular interest is the radio (how can we hear people talking far away through these speaker things?). After making many attempts to construct "crystal radios" out of razor blades and extra wire during elementary school, I finally got serious about my interest during my middle school years. Over the summer vacation between my eighth and ninth grade years (middle school and high school), I studied for and earned my amateur radio (ham radio) license.

When I expressed interest in becoming a ham radio operator, many adult operators in the community were more than happy to help me out. I was soon introduced to the local Ham Radio Club, and many of the adult members provided me with books, Morse code computer programs, and other materials to help me earn my license. In addition, they answered many questions that I had about the electrical and radio theory for the license.

As I continued to study radio and upgrade my license, my interest in ham radio spread to a more general interest in the field of electronics. Many ham radio operators design and construct their own equipment. Since I was in no position to buy fancy expensive radio equipment, I liked the idea of making some of my own. Having always liked the idea of taking junk and turning it into something useful, I figured there must be a way to rearrange the electronic parts in old TV sets, telephones, and other appliances to make them into working ham radios.

Through the Ham Radio Club, I met a man who had recently started his own small electronic design firm. He hired me over my vacations to do odd jobs around the shop. At work, he explained how his projects worked. The money I earned while working with him was nothing compared to what I learned from his projects and from watching his company grow. At first, I didn't understand the electrical terms and theories he showed me, but over time, I found myself trying to design my own projects in my makeshift shop at home. My own projects, needless to say, were not nearly as successful. My projects would go up in smoke half the time and would often seem to work better when I turned them off. From these experiences, I decided that I needed to go to college and learn what I was trying to do. I felt that I understood the basics of how electronics worked, but I did not have the depth that I needed to make my stuff actually work.

Pursue your interests and fulfill them. These interests may be the key to your future.

Index

About the Author

WILLIAM J. EKELER is editor of *The Black Student's Guide to College Success* (revised ed., 1995) and coeditor of the original edition (1993). A graduate of the University of Nebraska, he received a Master's degree in Education in administration, planning, and social policy from Harvard University. He also was director of student leadership activities at Radcliffe College. He is currently Director of Purchasing at Overland Products in Fremont, Nebraska.